Bloom's BioCritiques

Bloom's BioCritiques

HENRY DAVID THOREAU

Edited and with an introduction by
Harold Bloom
Sterling Professor of the Humanities
Yale University

CHELSEA HOUSE
P U B L I S H E R S
A Haights Cross Communications Company

Philadelphia

A Haights Cross Communications ✦ Company

Introduction © 2003 by Harold Bloom.

Printed and bound in the United States of America.

10 9 8 7 6 5 4 3 2 1

Library of Congress Cataloging-in-Publication Data
Applied for.
ISBN: 0-7910-6368-2

Chelsea House Publishers
1974 Sproul Road, Suite 400
Broomall, PA 19008-0914

http://www.chelseahouse.com

Contributing editor: Michael Cisco

Cover design by Keith Trego

Cover: © Bettman/CORBIS

Layout by EJB Publishing Services

CONTENTS

USER'S GUIDE

These volumes are designed to introduce the reader to the life and work of the world's literary masters. Each volume begins with Harold Bloom's essay "The Work in the Writer" and a volume-specific introduction also written by Professor Bloom. Following these unique introductions is an engaging biography that discusses the major life events and important literary accomplishments of the author under consideration.

Furthermore, each volume includes an original critique that not only traces the themes, symbols, and ideas apparent in the author's works, but strives to put those works into a cultural and historical perspective. In addition to the original critique is a brief selection of significant critical essays previously published on the author and his or her works followed by a concise and informative chronology of the writer's life. Finally, each volume concludes with a bibliography of the writer's works, a list of additional readings, and an index of important themes and ideas.

HAROLD BLOOM

The Work in the Writer

Literary biography found its masterpiece in James Boswell's *Life of Samuel Johnson*. Boswell, when he treated Johnson's writings, implicitly commented upon Johnson as found in his work, even as in the great critic's life. Modern instances of literary biography, such as Richard Ellmann's lives of W. B. Yeats, James Joyce, and Oscar Wilde, essentially follow in Boswell's pattern.

That the writer somehow is in the work, we need not doubt, though with William Shakespeare, writer-of-writers, we almost always need to rely upon pure surmise. The exquisite rancidities of the Problem Plays or Dark Comedies seem to express an extraordinary estrangement of Shakespeare from himself. When we read or attend *Troilus and Cressida* and *Measure for Measure*, we may be startled by particular speeches of Ulysses in the first play, or of Vincentio in the second. These speeches, of Ulysses upon hierarchy or upon time, or of Duke Vincentio upon death, are too strong either for their contexts or for the characters of their speakers. The same phenomenon occurs with Parolles, the military impostor of *All's Well That Ends Well*. Utterly disgraced, he nevertheless affirms: "Simply the thing I am/Shall make me live."

In Shakespeare, more even than in his peers, Dante and Cervantes, meaning always starts itself again through excess or overflow. The strongest of Shakespeare's creatures—Falstaff, Hamlet, Iago, Lear, Cleopatra—have an exuberance that is fiercer than their plays can contain. If Ben Jonson was at all correct in his complaint that "Shakespeare wanted art," it could have been only in a sense that he may not have intended. Where do the personalities of Falstaff or Hamlet touch a limit? What was it in Shakespeare that made the two parts of *Henry IV* and *Hamlet* into "plays unlimited"? Neither Falstaff nor Hamlet will be stopped: their wit, their beautiful, laughing speech, their intensity of being—all these are virtually infinite.

In what ways do Falstaff and Hamlet manifest the writer in the work? Evidently, we can never know, or know enough to answer with any authority. But what would happen if we reversed the question, and asked: How did the work form the writer, Shakespeare?

Of Shakespeare's inwardness, his biography tells us nothing. And yet, to an astonishing extent, Shakespeare created our inwardness. At the least, we can speculate that Shakespeare so lived his life as to conceal the depths of his nature, particularly as he rather prematurely aged. We do not have Shakespeare on Shakespeare, as any good reader of the Sonnets comes to realize: they do not constitute a key that unlocks his heart. No sequence of sonnets could be less confessional or more powerfully detached from the poet's self.

The German poet and universal genius, Goethe, affords a superb contrast to Shakespeare. Of Goethe's life, we know more than everything; I wonder sometimes if we know as much about Napoleon or Freud or any other human being who ever has lived, as we know about Goethe. Everywhere, we can find Goethe in his work, so much so that Goethe seems to crowd the writing out, just as Byron and Oscar Wilde seem to usurp their own literary accomplishments. Goethe, cunning beyond measure, nevertheless invested a rival exuberance in his greatest works that could match his personal charisma. The sublime outrageousness of the Second Part of *Faust*, or of the greater lyric and meditative poems, form a Counter-Sublime to Goethe's own daemonic intensity.

Goethe was fascinated by the daemonic in himself; we can doubt that Shakespeare had any such interests. Evidently, Shakespeare abandoned his acting career just before he composed *Measure for Measure* and *Othello*. I surmise that the egregious interventions by Vincentio and Iago displace the actor's energies into a new kind of mischief-making, a fresh opening to a subtler playwriting-within-the-play.

But what had opened Shakespeare to this new awareness? The answer is the work in the writer, *Hamlet* in Shakespeare. One can go further: it was not so much the play, *Hamlet*, as the character Hamlet, who changed Shakespeare's art forever.

Hamlet's personality is so large and varied that it rivals Goethe's own. Ironically Goethe's Faust, his Hamlet, has no personality at all, and is as colorless as Shakespeare himself seems to have chosen to be. Yet nothing could be more colorful than the Second Part of *Faust*, which is peopled by an astonishing array of monsters, grotesque devils, and classical ghosts.

A contrast between Shakespeare and Goethe demonstrates that in each—but in very different ways—we can better find the work in the person, than we can discover that banal entity, the person in the work. Goethe to many of his contemporaries, seemed to be a mortal god. Shakespeare, so far as we know, seemed an affable, rather ordinary fellow, who aged early and became somewhat withdrawn. Yet Faust, though Mephistopheles battles for his soul, is hardly worth the trouble unless you take him as an idea and not as a person. Hamlet is nearly every-idea-in-one, but he is precisely a personality and a person.

Would Hamlet be so astonishingly persuasive if his father's ghost did not haunt him? Falstaff is more alive than Prince Hal, who says that the devil haunts him in the shape of an old fat man. Three years before composing the final *Hamlet*, Shakespeare invented Falstaff, who then never ceased to haunt his creator. Falstaff and Hamlet may be said to best represent the work in the writer, because their influence upon Shakespeare was prodigious. W.H. Auden accurately observed that Falstaff possesses infinite energy: never tired, never bored, and absolutely both witty and happy until Hal's rejection destroys him. Hamlet too has infinite energy, but in him it is more curse than blessing.

Falstaff and Hamlet can be said to occupy the roles in Shakespeare's invented world that Sancho Panza and Don Quixote possess in Cervantes's. Shakespeare's plays from 1610 on (starting with *Twelfth Night*) are thus analogous to the Second Part of Cervantes's epic novel. Sancho and the Don overtly jostle Cervantes for authorship in the Second Part, even as Cervantes battles against the impostor who has pirated a continuation of his work. As a dramatist, Shakespeare manifests the work in the writer more indirectly. Falstaff's prose genius is revived in the scapegoating of Malvolio by Maria and Sir Toby Belch, while Falstaff's darker insights are developed by Feste's melancholic wit. Hamlet's intellectual resourcefulness, already deadly, becomes poisonous in Iago and in Edmund. Yet we have not crossed into the deeper abysses of the work in the writer in later Shakespeare.

No fictive character, before or since, is Falstaff's equal in self-trust. Sir John, whose delight in himself is contagious, has total confidence both in his self-awareness and in the resources of his language. Hamlet, whose self is as strong, and whose language is as copious, nevertheless distrusts both the self and language. Later Shakespeare is, as it were, much under the influence both of Falstaff and of Hamlet, but they tug him in opposite directions. Shakespeare's own copiousness of language is well-nigh incredible: a vocabulary in excess of twenty-one thousand words, almost eighteen hundred of which he coined himself. And of his word-hoard, nearly half are used only once each, as though the perfect setting for each had been found, and need not be repeated. Love for language and faith in language are Falstaffian attributes. Hamlet will darken both that love and that faith in Shakespeare, and perhaps the Sonnets can best be read as Falstaff and Hamlet counterpointing against one another.

Can we surmise how aware Shakespeare was of Falstaff and Hamlet, once they had played themselves into existence? *Henry IV, Part I* appeared in six quarto editions during Shakespeare's lifetime; *Hamlet* possibly had four. Falstaff and Hamlet were played again and again at the Globe, but Shakespeare knew also that they were being read, and he must have had contact with some of those readers. What would it have been like to discuss Falstaff or Hamlet with one of their early readers (presumably also part of their audience at the Globe), if you were the creator of such demiurges? The question would seem nonsensical to most Shakespeare scholars, but then these days they tend to be either ideologues or moldy figs. How can we recover the uncanniness of Falstaff and of Hamlet, when they now have become so familiar?

A writer's influence upon himself is an unexplored problem in criticism, but such an influence is never free from anxieties. The biocritical problem (which this series attempts to explore) can be divided into two areas, difficult to disengage fully. Accomplished works affect the author's life, and also affect her subsequent writings. It is simpler for me to surmise the effect of *Mrs. Dalloway* and *To the Lighthouse* upon Woolf's late *Between the Acts*, than it is to relate Clarissa Dalloway's suicide and Lily Briscoe's capable endurance in art to the tragic death and complex life of Virginia Woolf.

There are writers whose lives were so vivid that they seem sometimes to obscure the literary achievement: Byron, Wilde, Malraux, Hemingway. But most major Western writers do not live that exuberantly, and the greatest of all, Shakespeare, sometimes appears to have adopted the personal mask of colorlessness. And yet there are heroes of literature who struggled titanically with their own eras— Tolstoy, Milton, Victor Hugo—who nevertheless matter more for their works than their lives.

There are great figures—Emily Dickinson, Wallace Stevens, Willa Cather—who seem to have had so little of the full intensity of life when compared to the vitality of their work, that we might almost speak of the work in the work, rather than even of the work in a person. Emily Brontë might well be the extreme instance of such a visionary, surpassing William Blake in that one regard.

I conclude this general introduction to a series of literary bio-critiques by stating a tentative formula or principle for gauging the many ways in which the work influences the person and her subsequent, later work. Our influence upon ourselves is always related to the Shakespearean invention of self-overhearing, which I have written about in several other contexts. Life, as well as poetry and prose, is overheard rather than simply heard. The writer listens to herself as though she were somebody else, and the will to change begins to operate. The forces that live in us include the prior work we have done, and the dreams and waking visions that evade our dismissals.

HAROLD BLOOM

Introduction

Thoreau professed to lead his life by acting out his ideas. Chapter 2 of *Walden* (1854) is "Where I Lived, and What I Lived For." Few declarations in American literature are as famous as this:

> I went to the woods because I wished to live deliberately, to front only the essential facts of life, and see if I could not learn what it had to teach, and not, when I came to die, discover that I had not lived. I did not wish to live what was not life, living is so dear; nor did I wish to practise resignation, unless it was quite necessary. I wanted to live deep and suck out all the marrow of life, to live so sturdily and Spartan-like as to put to rout all that was not life, to cut a broad swath and shave close, to drive life into a corner, and reduce it to its lowest terms, and, if it proved to be mean, why then to get the whole and genuine meanness of it, and publish its meanness to the world; or if it were sublime, to know it by experience, and be able to give a true account of it in my next excursion.

For Thoreau then, work and life are a theory of fusion. Such fusion depends upon a radical isolation: from the post office, the newspaper, or in our day, the screen of all varieties:

For my part, I could easily do without the post-office. I think that there are very few important communications made through it. To speak critically, I never received more than one or two letters in my life—I wrote this some years ago— that were worth the postage. The penny-post is, commonly, an institution through which you seriously offer a man that penny for his thoughts which is so often safely offered in jest. And I am sure that I never read any memorable news in a newspaper. If we read of one man robbed, or murdered, or killed by accident, or one house burned or one vessel wrecked, or one steamboat blown up, or one cow run over on the Western Railroad, or one mad dog killed, or one lot of grasshoppers in the winter—we never need read another. One is enough. If you are acquainted with the principle, what do you care for a myriad instances and applications?

I myself, though an admirer of Emerson much more than of Thoreau, have in my old age mostly given up reading *The New York Times*, particularly when the baseball season has passed. It is not that fresh catastrophes lack vividness, but that, as W.B. Yeats wrote: "Things thought too long can be no longer thought." Now, in the autumn of 2002, what is best to be learned from the effect of Thoreau's writings upon his life?

From his mentor, Ralph Waldo Emerson, the young Thoreau had learned that his true quest was to "enjoy an original relationship to the universe." The medium of this relation, its sphere and its active agent, was eloquence, the interior oratory of which Emerson was the master. Transcendentalism was, for Thoreau, an entire culture, a program to realize. Thoreau may be regarded as the pragmatist of Transcendentalism.

Still, Thoreau was a rather disconcerting pragmatist: like Walt Whitman, whom he admired, Thoreau proceeded to loaf and invite his soul. What except writing could be an appropriate vocation for a Transcendentalist? An essentially literary movement could not produce merchants, bankers, lawyers, politicians, clergymen.

Emerson, in his beautiful, elegiac essay on Thoreau, seems puzzled that his disciple so literalized solitude. And yet Thoreau hardly thought of himself as a hermit. For him, his famous sojourn at Walden Pond had a societal purpose. Thoreau wants us to learn from him never to pay a penny more—monetary or spiritual—for anything than it is worth. That is a remarkable principle: can any of us still hope to live by it? Should we, even if possible?

Thoreau wrote that "he is the true artist whose life is his material," which Sherman Paul juxtaposes with Thoreau's famous couplet:

> My life hath been the poem I would have writ,
> But I could not both live and live to utter it.

That indeed so fuses life and poem that the limits of discourse are strained. But then it is the genius of Thoreau to bruise the relation between social existence and individual thought. He confided to his Journal that his endless friendship with Emerson was one long tragedy. Neither man could be termed an exuberant personality, but precursor and strong revisionist only rarely have managed to exist together.

Thoreau's particular favorite among Walt Whitman's poems was "Crossing Brooklyn Ferry," presumably because it is a hymn to the future, like its descendant, Hart Crane's *The Bridge*. It seems curious to think of Thoreau as a prophet, because the element of renunciation in him is so large: and yet hear the closing paragraph of the fierce essay, "Life Without Principle":

> Those things which now most engage the attention of men, as politics and the daily routine, are, it is true, vital functions of human society, but should be unconsciously performed, like the corresponding functions of the physical body. They are *infra*-human, a kind of vegetation. I sometimes awake to a half-consciousness of them going on about me, as a man may become conscious of some of the processes of digestion in a morbid state, and so have the dyspepsia, as it is called. It is as if a thinker submitted himself to be rasped by the great gizzard of creation. Politics is, as it were, the gizzard of society, full of grit and gravel, and the two political parties are its two opposite halves—sometimes split into quarters, it may be, which grind on each other. Not only individuals, but states, have thus a confirmed dyspepsia, which expresses itself, you can imagine by what sort of eloquence. Thus our life is not altogether a forgetting, but also, alas! to a great extent, a remembering, of that which we should never have been conscious of, certainly not in our waking hours. Why should we not meet, not always as

dyspeptics, to tell our bad dreams, but sometimes as *eu*peptics, to congratulate each other on the ever-glorious morning? I do not make an exorbitant demand, surely.

The ironies here, with their Wordsworthian echoes, are surely prophetic. "Civil Disobedience," Thoreau's most influential essay, concludes more urgently:

The authority of government, even such as I am willing to submit to—for I will cheerfully obey those who know and can do better than I, and in many things even those who neither know nor can do so well—is still an impure one: to be strictly just, it must have the sanction and consent of the governed. It can have no pure right over my person and property but what I concede to it. The progress from an absolute to a limited monarchy, from a limited monarchy to a democracy, is a progress toward a true respect for the individual. Even the Chinese philosopher was wise enough to regard the individual as the basis of the empire. Is a democracy, such as we know it, the last improvement possible in government? Is it not possible to take a step further towards recognizing and organizing the rights of man? There will never be a really free and enlightened State until the State comes to recognize the individual as a higher and independent power, from which all its own power and authority are derived, and treats him accordingly. I please myself with imagining a State at last which can afford to be just to all men, and to treat the individual with respect as a neighbor; which even would not think it inconsistent with its own repose if a few were to live aloof from it, not meddling with it, nor embraced by it, who fulfilled all the duties of neighbors and fellow-men. A State which bore this kind of fruit, and suffered it to drop off as fast as it ripened, would prepare the way for a still more perfect and glorious State, which also I have imagined, but not yet seen anywhere.

This is altogether visionary, in the year 2002. Thoreau remains a beacon, and yet we drift farther and farther away from him. None of us now can hope so strenuously to fuse life and work.

ELLYN SANNA

Biography of Henry David Thoreau

Escape from Civilization

Henry David Thoreau was happiest when he was alone in the woods. For Thoreau, nature was the source of his deepest literary and spiritual inspiration, and Walden Pond, two miles south of the village of Concord, had been one of his favorite natural spots since childhood. So, when he decided that he needed a place to appreciate nature in solitude, Thoreau chose to build a home beside Walden Pond, on land that belonged to his friend Ralph Waldo Emerson.

In the spring of 1845, Thoreau began clearing a site in the pine woods beside Walden Pond for his cabin. By mid-April, he had the house framed and ready to construct; in early May, many of his neighbors joined him for the house-raising. He moved in on July 4, 1845.

While Thoreau's new home provided him with the solitude he required, it was by no means a lonely place, being within easy walking distance of both his parents' home and Concord village. He furnished it simply with a caned bed, a table, a desk, and three chairs, and equipped it with a three-inch mirror and a washbowl, a pair of tongs, andirons, and a lamp. Utensils were minimal: a kettle, a skillet, a frying pan, a dipper, a cup, a spoon, two knives and forks, three plates, and jugs for oil and molasses. Most of the furnishings he made himself. As cold weather set in, Thoreau winterized the house by adding plaster and laths to the walls. He also built a fireplace and chimney.

Thoreau realized he needed more than just a habitation in which to write; he also needed to change the way he lived his life. Work six days and rest the seventh, the Bible instructed, but Thoreau decided to do the reverse: in an effort to simplify his life, he would work one day a week and rest for six. For Thoreau, "resting" meant writing and observing nature.

When not engaged in writing or immersed in nature, Thoreau worked in his garden. It was a success the first year, and he sold what he did not use himself; after deducting his expenses of $14.73 for tools, seeds, and a cultivator, he realized a profit of $8.71.

Thoreau earned a living by performing odd jobs such as fence building, house painting, gardening, and carpentry; he was hired for a variety of projects, including the construction of a fireplace and a woodshed. He also used his skills as a surveyor to earn money, and these jobs gave him special pleasure—they allowed him to earn money while at the same time enjoying the fields and woods he loved.

During his time on Walden Pond, Thoreau found many ways to fascinate and entertain his curiosity. Using a fishing line, a stone weighing one and a half pounds, a compass, and a chain, he measured the depth of the pond, which was in actuality a small glacial lake, only three-quarters of a mile in length and half a mile in width. A century later, a trained limnologist verified Thoreau's findings. He also conducted his own studies on Walden and compiled various statistics that he compared with other ponds, rivers, and springs.

Thoreau loved every aspect of the natural world. A friend later recalled a visit with Thoreau at Walden Pond:

> "Keep very still and I will show you my family," Thoreau suddenly said to him, and then he stepped quickly outside the cabin door and gave a low whistle. A woodchuck responded to the call, running toward him from a nearby burrow. With another whistle, he summoned a pair of gray squirrels that exhibited no fear as they ran up to him. Then he gave still another whistle, and several birds, including two crows, flew toward him; one of the crows settled comfortably on his shoulder. Thoreau fed all the animals with food from his pocket and gently petted them.

Another visitor, Mary Hosmer Brown, recorded her mother's memories of her visits to Walden Pond: "To take a walk with Thoreau, one must rigidly adhere to the manners of the woods. He could lead one to the ripest berries, the hidden nest, the rarest flowers, but no plant life could be carelessly destroyed, no mother bird lose her eggs."

Thoreau had a favorite mouse that had a nest under his house. At first, it came out when he ate his lunch and picked up the crumbs that fell around his feet, but as it grew accustomed to him, it became so trusting that it ran over his shoes and through the inside of his pants; when he held out a piece of cheese, it nibbled it from his fingers. One of the few decorations Thoreau permitted in his cabin was a drawing on the closet door depicting him with his pet mouse.

Thoreau kept busy observing nature, gardening, working, and visiting with friends, but he spent most of his time writing, which was the reason why he had sought the isolation of the woods in the first place.

THOREAU'S BEGINNINGS

David Henry Thoreau was born in his maternal grandmother's farmhouse on Virginia Road in Concord, Massachusetts, on July 12, 1817. Concord was a rural community, an agricultural town with a population of about two thousand people. The national climate at the time of Thoreau's birth was one of peace and relief, since the country had only recently recovered from the War of 1812. James Monroe had just been inaugurated as president in 1817, beginning the period of tranquility and prosperity known as "the era of good feeling."

The Thoreau family's affairs were not quite as prosperous as the nation's. After a series of physical, political, and financial misfortunes, they were trying—unsuccessfully—to regain their earlier lofty status in the community at the time of Henry's birth.

Henry's family originated from courageous stock—men and women of principle who remained stalwart in their convictions even when they were in the minority. The Thoreau family was of French Protestant ancestry, but they had relocated to the Isle of Jersey in the English Channel after 1685 for religious reasons. In 1773 Jean Thoreau, Henry's grandfather, was the first in the family to come to America.

Mary Jones Dunbar, Henry's maternal grandmother and the only grandparent he ever knew, was born into a family of British Loyalists who had been held in the Concord jail during the Revolution; Mary, assisting her family members with information and horses, had succeeded in helping them escape to Loyalist Canada. After her first husband's death, she operated a tavern from her home in Keene until she married Captain Jonas Minott in 1798 and settled on his farm on Virginia Road in Concord. She was widowed again in 1813 and moved into the village, where she eventually shared her home with her daughter's family.

Henry's father, John Thoreau, was born in Boston, Massachusetts, on October 8, 1787. He moved to Concord in 1800 and clerked in a couple of stores until he came of age. He then mortgaged his father's estate to open his own store with a business partner, but then dissolved the business when he and his partner quarreled. He married Cynthia Dunbar in 1812, and also served as commissary at Fort Independence in Boston Harbor during the War of 1812, a service for which he received 160 acres of land. He eventually took over the management of a store in Concord Center.

John Thoreau was very musical; he enjoyed reading the classics, and handed down many of his books to his son Henry. A good-natured, lovable man, John was quiet and unassuming.

Henry's mother, on the other hand, was a woman with a strong, dynamic personality who played an active part in Concord society. She was a member of the Female Charitable Society and the Bible Society and, despite her family's own poverty, she assisted the downtrodden. A born reformer, she was outspoken on moral issues; she was one of the founders of the Concord Women's Anti-Slavery Society.

Both of Henry's parents had an interest in nature that they shared with their children. The family spent much of their time exploring the banks of the Assabet River, the cliffs at Fairhaven, and the shores of Walden Pond.

Henry was the third of John and Cynthia's four children. He had two sisters—Helen, who was the eldest, born in 1812, and Sophia, born in 1819; John Jr., a charming and outgoing boy who was considered the more promising of the two boys, was born in 1815.

Shortly after Henry's birth, the family's financial situation worsened. John, in poor health, was forced to sign over his share in the family home, which he had mortgaged in Boston years before to compensate the attorney who made the final settlement of the Thoreau estate. In 1818, the Virginia Road house, where Henry was born, was also sold by court order. Henry and his family moved into the village, where they rented the western half of Red House at 201 Lexington Road, where Cynthia's mother resided. John Thoreau's health improved, and in 1818 he again opened a grocery store.

As young boys, Henry and his brother John slept together in a trundle bed. While John fell asleep at once, Henry often lay awake. When his mother asked him, "Why Henry dear, don't you go to sleep?" he replied, "Mother, I have been looking through the stars to see if I could see God behind them."

Thoreau's youngest sister Sophia later taught school, as did their sister Helen. Sophia appears to have inherited some of her mother's high-minded convictions. According to one story, she stalked out of church rather than accept the communion for which she could not believe. When their father died, Sophia helped manage the family business, even though women were not readily accepted in matters outside of the domestic circle. She also edited Thoreau's unpublished manuscripts after his death.

By 1821 John Thoreau's attempts at storekeeping had failed again. Apparently he was too kind-hearted to refuse credit to his customers, and he could not bring himself to collect money owed to him. The family moved to Boston, where Henry's father taught school for a time. It was in Boston that Henry started school, at age five.

While living in Boston, Henry visited his grandmother in Concord, where he made his first visit to Walden Pond. He wrote these lines to describe the experience:

> One of the most ancient scenes stamped on the tablets of my memory ... That sweet solitude my spirit seemed so early to require at once gave the preference to this recess among the pines, where almost sunshine and shadow were the only inhabitants that varied the scene, over that tumultuous and varied city, as if it had found its proper nursery.

From very early in his life, he associated Walden Pond with his happiest moments.

Henry's uncle, Charles Dunbar, a lifelong bachelor, was also a wanderer who traveled wherever he felt inclined to go. He often lived with the Thoreaus, but the family never knew when Uncle Charles would leave on a whim and disappear for months, only to reappear once again entirely unannounced. Despite his lack of predictability, Charles helped Henry's family finally achieve financial security when he discovered a graphite deposit while traveling through Bristol, New Hampshire. He staked out a claim and under the firm name of Dunbar & Stow, he and his partner began working the claim, which contained the finest quality of graphite in the United States. By 1824, both Charles and his partner dropped out of the business, and the firm was renamed John Thoreau & Company. Because of the superior quality of his pencils, Thoreau's father received a special citation from the Massachusetts Agricultural Society.

When the family returned to Concord, Henry was enrolled in Miss Phoebe Wheeler's private "infant" school, where he learned his ABCs. From there he went on to public grammar school on the common, the same school where he himself would later teach for a brief time. Much of Thoreau's education there consisted of memorizing passages from the Bible, Shakespeare, Bunyan, Johnson, and the famous English essayists. Because the public school sessions were so short, Mrs. Thoreau often sent her sons to Phoebe Wheeler's school for girls for some additional education.

Henry was rather quiet and solemn, content to remain on the sidelines at school while his brother John entertained their classmates with stories. Very early in his life, Henry developed a reputation for being stoical and self-contained. When he sold several pet chickens to an inn and the innkeeper slaughtered them in front of him, Henry made not a single sound or gesture to express his shock and distress. When he was accused of stealing a knife from a schoolmate, he replied only, "I did not take it." After a few days the culprit was found, and Henry revealed that he had known all the time who had taken the knife, and reminded his accusers that he had been in Newton with his father on the day it was stolen. When asked why he did not say this at the time he was accused, he only said again, "I did not take it."

As a boy, Henry relished the days when he was allowed to stay home from school to pick huckleberries on a neighboring hill. Such days, he thought, were "like the promise of life eternal."

His mother often took her children into the yard to listen to the songs of wild birds. On bright afternoons, they walked out to Nashawtuc

Hill or the cliffs at Fairhaven, or built a campfire in the patch of woods between the river and Main Street and cooked their supper while enjoying the flowers and birdsongs.

Henry dreaded the long Puritan Sundays, when he was compelled to stay inside the house without even the diversion of an interesting book. On these Sunday afternoons, he spent hours looking from an attic window at the martins soaring around their box. If an occasional hawk appeared in the sky, he was all the more delighted; it took his thoughts, he said, "from earthly things."

In 1828, when Henry was eleven years old, he and his brother were enrolled in the Concord Academy, where they were instructed by Phineas Allen. The fee for academy instruction was $5 per quarter per pupil, which was a sacrifice for the Thoreau family at the time, but Cynthia Thoreau felt strongly that her sons should receive the best education possible. Mr. Allen emphasized the classics, including Virgil, Cicero, Euripides, Homer, Voltaire, Molière, and Racine, all taught in their original languages. He also taught geography, history, grammar, spelling, astronomy, botany, algebra, trigonometry, geometry, natural philosophy, and natural history, placing a special emphasis on composition and frequent theme paper assignments.

Henry had little interest in school, but he enjoyed the Concord Lyceum, which had been established in 1829 as part of the "lyceum movement" that arose in the mid-1820s. The Lyceum hosted concerts, lectures, and debates on scientific, moral, and historical issues; it offered an intellectual outlet and stimulus for the rural and somewhat isolated area, and was an important part of Thoreau's education. Lyceum topics included geology, botany, and ornithology, which probably influenced Thoreau's interests in these areas.

Thoreau was most interested in the outdoors, and he spent much of his spare time in Concord's woods and meadows and on her rivers and ponds. Among other boys his age, he was known as the one "who did not fear mud or water, nor paused to lift his followers over the ditch." For the most part, Thoreau left little impression on his schoolmates at the Concord Academy. In the words of one, he was "an odd stick, not very studious or devoted in his lessons, but a thoughtful youth and very fond of reading ... not given to play or fellowship with the boys; but shy and silent."

In the summer of 1833, after his last quarter at the Academy, he devoted his spare time to the building of his first boat, a rowboat he christened *The Rover*, in which he further explored the ponds and rivers of Concord. He spent many happy hours floating on Walden Pond, rowing his boat out to the middle and then lying on his back across the seats and daydreaming. When he felt the boat touch the sand, he would rouse himself to see where he had floated. On lazy days like these, he thought "idleness was the most attractive and productive industry."

Although his brother John was considered more intelligent, Thoreau was more studious. In the summer of 1833, he took his entrance exams for admission to Harvard. He only barely passed, and he required "conditioning," or tutoring, in Greek, Latin, and mathematics before he was admitted into the university. This was not an unusual requirement; the Harvard entrance exam was so difficult that more than 90 percent of the students who took it were required to have "conditioning" in at least one subject.

The Thoreaus did not have enough money to send both Henry and his brother John to Harvard, but their mother wanted one of her sons to follow in her father's footsteps and attend Harvard, so she asked the extended family to help with the $179 per year for Henry's tuition. The pencil business had begun to prosper; Helen and John contributed from their teaching salaries, and even Henry's aunts pitched in. On August 30, 1833, Henry and his friend Charles Stearns Wheeler traveled to Cambridge together, and there they became roommates.

At the time Thoreau attended Harvard, there were only thirty-five faculty members, among them Henry Wadsworth Longfellow. Edward Tyrell Channing, professor of rhetoric and oratory, was the professor who most influenced Thoreau. Channing helped Thoreau achieve a personal style and learn to express himself.

In May of 1834, the end of Thoreau's freshman year, a full-scale uprising took place on the Harvard campus when a student of Greek refused to continue a recitation for his instructor, Christopher Dunkin, and told him, "I do not recognize your authority," giving rise to the riot later referred to as the Dunkin Rebellion. The classroom itself was destroyed later that evening, and other disruptions and mischief disturbed the normally peaceful campus. The college president was unable to bring order; eventually, he expelled the entire sophomore class for the rest of the year, with the exception of three students. The mischief-makers were readmitted the following school year only after they had taken new examinations and presented the college with certificates of good conduct.

One of the leaders of the rebellion, John Weiss, said that during the uproar Thoreau:

> had no animal spirits for our sport or mischief. We cannot recollect what became of him during the scenes of the Dunkin Rebellion. He must have slipped off into some "cool retreat or mossy cell." We are half inclined to suppose that the tumult startled him into some metamorphose, that corresponded to a yearning in him of some natural kind, whereby he secured a temporary evasion till peace was restored ... Thoreau disappeared while our young absurdity held its orgies, stripping shutters from the lower windows of the buildings, dismantling recitation rooms, greeting tutors and professors with a frenzied and groundless indignation which we symbolized by kindling the spoils of sacked premises upon the steps. It probably occurred to him that fools might rush in where angels were not in the habit of going.

Of the sixty-three boys who were members of Thoreau's class, he was one of only nineteen that never got into trouble throughout their entire college careers.

During Thoreau's time at college he consistently achieved above-average grades, and on a few occasions he was awarded "exhibition money" for his excellent work. During his junior and senior years, he missed a good deal of school due to illness, and during the second term of his junior year he dropped out of the university for a few months in order to earn money by teaching school. His illness that same year may have been the beginning of his lifelong struggle with tuberculosis.

Thoreau returned to Harvard after two months away. He was thrilled to have access to the university's large library, and since his schoolwork did not take up all his time, he did a great deal of reading for his own pleasure and interest. While at Harvard he began his practice of carrying notebooks to jot down whatever quotations from great poets and authors struck his fancy. From these collections he drew many of the quotations for the essays he wrote in the 1840s.

Thoreau graduated on August 30, 1837. His good grades entitled him to a part in the commencement exercises, and he spoke about the value of nature to the human spirit:

Let men, true to their natures, cultivate the moral affections, lead manly and independent lives; let them make riches the means and not the end of existence, and we shall hear no more of the commercial spirit. The sea will not stagnate, the earth will be as green as ever, and the air as pure. This curious world which we inhabit is more wonderful than convenient; more beautiful than it is useful; it is more to be admired and enjoyed than used. The order of things should be somewhat reversed; the seventh should be man's day of toil, wherein to earn his living by the sweat of his brow; and the other six his Sabbath of the affections and the soul—in which to range this widespread garden, and drink in the soft influences and sublime revelations of nature.

OPPORTUNITIES AND DISAPPOINTMENTS

After his graduation, Thoreau was faced with the decision of choosing a profession. The four avenues open to a college graduate during that time period were the ministry, law, medicine, or teaching; without hesitation, Thoreau chose teaching. He was immediately offered a position at the Center School in Concord, which he himself had attended as a child, with a salary of $500 per year.

Thoreau soon encountered difficulty in his teaching career. Enrollment at the school was high and included several difficult students who were not serious about their studies. After Thoreau had been teaching for two weeks, a member of the school committee came to observe his class, and concluded that Thoreau's failure to use corporal punishment to keep the students in line would "spoil the school." Upset by the criticism, Thoreau decided he would rather work at an academy or private school where he could teach the way he saw fit, and he resigned to a member of the school committee that same evening.

The townspeople were dismayed by Thoreau's decision, not understanding why anyone would give up perfectly good employment so quickly, especially in a time of economic depression. They decided he was an odd sort when he suddenly began to refer to himself as "Henry David" rather than by his given name of "David Henry." His family had always called him Henry, however, and he thought the reversed names sounded better. Although he never had his name changed legally, for the rest of his life he continued to sign his name "Henry David."

Thoreau found teaching jobs scarce, and he had not helped his cause by voluntarily giving up a position. When he was unable to find another job, he worked for a while in his father's pencil factory. He had little interest in manufacturing, but he did develop a few innovations that were responsible for greatly improving the product.

American pencil leads could be very gritty; compared to the lead found in Faber pencils imported from Germany, they were of poor quality. Doing some research in the Harvard Library, Thoreau discovered that German manufacturers mixed their graphite with fine Bavarian clay and then baked it, thus creating a harder and blacker lead. Since the American lead was still gritty, Henry designed a grinding mill to refine the graphite further.

During the first winter after his graduation, Thoreau developed what would become the most important friendship of his life. Ralph Waldo Emerson was another intellectual with whom Thoreau could share his thoughts and from whom he could receive guidance. The two men shared a bond that was almost a father-son relationship. Emerson also had a large personal library he made available to Thoreau. In many ways, the older man acted as an intellectual catalyst, inspiring Thoreau with new ideas and intellectual growth. Emerson and Thoreau shared religious beliefs as well.

John Locke's rational approach to religion had caused many to reject the concept of the Trinity—God the Father, God the Son, and God the Spirit—in favor of a Unitarian Christianity that emphasized God's oneness. Locke's world was one that depended on the senses for proof (the scientific method was another of his philosophical legacies), but by the late 1700s, Kant and Hegel from Germany were advancing their own philosophies. These theories granted some validity to Locke's ideas while contending that human beings possessed an innate body of knowledge that transcended the senses. This knowledge was the voice of God within human beings—their conscience, their moral sense, their inner light, their over-soul. This new form of religious faith was called Transcendentalism.

Transcendentalists believed that all children were born with the ability to distinguish between right and wrong, but that, as children grew older, they tended to listen to the world about them rather than the voice within them, and their moral sense became calloused. This was the Transcendentalists' explanation for evil in the world. It was the duty of good people to return to a state of childish innocence where they could once more hear the voice of God within them.

These ideas had spread to New England by the mid 1830s through Samuel Taylor Coleridge and Thomas Carlyle. While attending a bicentennial celebration at Harvard, a group of alumni, including Emerson, Thoreau, and a few others, discovered they shared a belief in many of these principles, a realization that prompted them to form the "Hedge Club." (Reverend Frederick Hedge was one of the members, and the meetings were generally scheduled so that he would be able to travel from his home in Bangor, Maine, and attend meetings in Emerson's home in Concord, where most of the club's meetings were held.) Thoreau was younger than the other members, but he was more consistent and passionate in his Transcendentalism than many of the older members, and he remained so throughout his life.

During his lifetime and for some time after, Thoreau was often considered to be an imitator of Emerson. The two men did in fact share nearly identical backgrounds, which may have contributed to their similar ideas. Emerson, however, regarded his friend Thoreau as a true original. He was always generous in his praise and appreciation of Thoreau: "In reading [Thoreau]," Emerson said, "I find the same thoughts, the same spirit that is in me."

Thoreau had great admiration and respect for another writer as well—Bronson Alcott, the father of Louisa May Alcott. The admiration was mutual; constantly amazed at the breadth of Thoreau's knowledge about nature, Alcott wrote that Thoreau possessed the ability "to see round the corner of himself, to comprehend everything."

Thoreau was published for the first time in the *Yeoman's Gazette* on November 25, 1837, when he wrote an obituary for Anna Jones, a woman he had visited in the Concord Poorhouse prior to her death. She had been the last person alive who could recall events of the Revolutionary War. The piece was printed anonymously and was not identified as Thoreau's until the mid-1900s.

Still more important from a literary standpoint was the journal that Thoreau began to keep in the fall of 1837. He continued to write in his journal faithfully, almost daily, for the next twenty-four years until his death. This journal may have been Thoreau's major literary accomplishment, but its excessive length of nearly two million words, amounting to more than seven thousand pages, kept it from becoming as popular as *Walden* or "Civil Disobedience."

In his journal, Thoreau discussed methods of writing, editing, and revising, and recorded much of the information he used in his later writings: his observations, reflections, musings, and quotations. In fact, his early journal was used in such a practical way that he actually cut out selections he intended to use for his essays or books. What was left over he recopied into a volume he called "Gleanings or What Time Has Not Reaped of My Journal."

The Concord Lyceum was another avenue that allowed Thoreau to test his ideas on others. He first appeared on the platform on April 11, 1838, offering his thoughts on "Society" and stating that "society was made for man," rather than the other way around. "The mass never comes up to the standard of its best member, but on the contrary degrades itself to a level with the lowest."

By the fall of 1838, Thoreau had been elected to the positions of secretary and curator of the Lyceum, duties he carried out until December of 1840. As curator, he was responsible for making arrangements for lectures and securing a site where they would be held.

Another important influence in the Thoreau household—and in Henry's life—was the presence of Mrs. Joseph Ward and her daughters Prudence and Caroline. Mrs. Ward was the widow of a Revolutionary War colonel who met Henry's maiden aunts Elizabeth, Jane, and Maria Thoreau in Boston, and moved to Concord in 1833 with Prudence to live with them. When the women's Anti-Slavery Society was formed in Concord in 1837, Mrs. Ward, along with Henry's mother and his sisters, became charter members.

The abolitionist movement was not yet popular, even in the North, but even so, the Concord women's organization grew to more than one hundred members. By 1839, it did more to support abolitionist causes such as William Lloyd Garrison's than any other similar organization in New England. The Society's sympathies also extended to the mistreatment of the Cherokee Indians in Georgia, and they persuaded Ralph Waldo Emerson to write a letter to President Martin Van Buren on their behalf. These courageous women's activities and ideas were an important part of Thoreau's developing thoughts.

Although Thoreau kept busy intellectually, after a year's fruitless search, he still had not found another teaching position. In mid-June of

1838 he decided to open his own private school in his family's home, the Parkman House on Main Street, where students could also board, if necessary. By late summer, the master at the Concord Academy had resigned and Thoreau made arrangements to rent that building for $5 per quarter. He placed an advertisement for his new school in the newspaper, but responses were few; by October, he was discouraged and considered seeking other employment.

However, by the end of the term the school's enrollment had grown so much that his brother John gave up his school in Roxbury to join Henry, teaching English and elementary mathematics in the lower level of the schoolhouse while Henry taught Latin, Greek, French, physics, natural philosophy, and natural history in the upstairs hall. Soon they reached their maximum enrollment of twenty-five students and had to start a waiting list. Most of their students came from Concord; among them was Bronson Alcott's daughter Louisa May.

The Thoreaus had their own philosophies regarding teaching and discipline, which included a contract between the students and the instructors. They took aside students who decided to enroll in the school and asked them what they wanted to study and what they hoped to gain from the experience. After hearing a student's desires, Henry or John replied:

> If you really wish to study those things, we can teach you, if you will obey our rules and promise to give your mind to your studies; but if you come to idle and play, or to see other boys study, we shall not want you for a pupil. Do you promise, then, to do what we require? If so, we will do our best to teach you what we know ourselves.

Any students who did not fulfill their end of the bargain were reminded by the Thoreau brothers that they had broken their word. To maintain strict discipline while avoiding the harsh physical punishment that was so common in most other school settings, the brothers also assigned duties for each student to perform during leisure time, to prevent mischief-making.

On one occasion, when a boy was overheard swearing, Henry Thoreau gathered all the students together and reasoned with them, explaining that such communication was silly and ineffective. "Boys," he returned home to Concord to continue their silent competition, sending Ellen gifts and writing her letters. Ellen returned to Concord for a visit the following June, and when she returned home, John followed her. He visited her yet again that July—to propose to her.

She accepted, but then soon realized that she actually preferred Henry to John. In any case, her mother convinced her to break off the engagement. Ellen's father would not have approved of either of the Thoreaus as a husband for his daughter; they were too "Transcendentalist" for his taste.

Henry tried his own proposal in November. This time Ellen consulted her father before replying, and agreed that it would be best if she refused Henry's proposal. Years later Ellen told her children that "she had been so distressed and had felt so mortified and worried over her mistaken acceptance of John and the consequent trouble and disturbance that she could only acquiesce in her father's desire with regard to Henry." She remained friends with his family, and asked for news about him for the rest of his life.

Thoreau did not forget Ellen, either. Two months after his rejection, he complained in his journal: "To sigh under the cold cold moon for a love unrequited, is to put a slight upon nature; the natural remedy would be to fall in love with the moon and the night, and find our love requited." The next day he added: "Disappointment will make us conversant with the nobler part of our nature." Years later, he told his sister Sophia, "I have always loved her. I have always loved her."

Although he never married, Thoreau did not give up easily on love. During the summers of 1840 and 1841, Mary Russell, from Plymouth, Massachusetts, a woman three years his junior, resided with the Emersons while employed as a tutor and governess for the Emersons' son Waldo. Thoreau was also living with the Emersons during the summer of 1841, and spent much time in Mary's company. When she returned home to Plymouth that fall, he wrote a poem for her called "To the Maiden in the East." A couple of weeks later, he wrote an entry in his journal that may have been addressed to her:

> It is not easy to find one brave enough to play the game of love quite alone with you, but they must get some third person, or world, to countenance them. They thrust others between. Love is so delicate and fastidious that I see not how

said, "if you went to talk business with a man, and he persisted in thrusting words having no connection with the subject into all parts of every sentence—Boot-jack, for instance—wouldn't you think he was taking a liberty with you, and trifling with your time, and wasting his own?" Henry then used the word bootjack inappropriately and violently in a sentence, as a demonstration of the silliness of profanity.

In the summer of 1839, between their summer and fall sessions, Henry and John planned a vacation—a boat trip on the Concord and Merrimack Rivers, with an excursion afterward to the White Mountains. They equipped their boat, the *Musketaquid* (the Indian name for the Concord River), with two sets of oars, two masts, sails, and a pair of wheels that would enable them to roll the boat around any falls they encountered. They also took along several poles to push the boat through shallow water, and a cotton tent that they hung on one of the masts to provide shelter for the night.

For two weeks they enjoyed their adventure, admiring the wonders of nature, visiting friends in Concord and New Hampshire, and climbing to the summit of Mount Washington, the highest of the White Mountains.

For the rest of his life, Thoreau would remember the voyage he and his brother took on the Concord and Merrimack rivers, a trip that grew in significance in Thoreau's mind as the years passed. After his brother's death, as Thoreau remembered the experience, he applied to the vacation a deeper meaning; it became a nearly tangible symbol of Thoreau's love and admiration for his lost brother, a symbol that he eventually transformed into his first book, *A Week on the Concord and Merrimack Rivers*.

Not only did Thoreau have a pleasant adventure with his brother in the summer of 1839, but he also fell in love with seventeen-year-old Ellen Sewall, who arrived in Concord in July for a two-week visit with the Wards and Thoreaus. Thoreau had met Ellen before, but she had now grown into a beautiful young woman. With John and their Aunt Prudence, Henry spent many happy hours with Ellen, walking, sailing, picking berries, riding, talking, and entertaining each other. Thoreau wrote her poems that hinted of his love for her. Ellen remembered their time together as some of the happiest moments of her life.

John shared Henry's feelings for Ellen. The two brothers, along with their Aunt Prudence, visited Ellen at Christmastime and then

[it] can ever begin. Do you expect me to love with you, unless you make my love secondary to nothing else? Your words come tainted as if the thought of the world darted between thee and the thought of me. You are not venturous enough for love. It goes along unscathed through wildernesses ...

Did I ask thee to love me who hate myself? No! Love that I love, and I will love thee that lovest.

Although Thoreau was unsuccessful in love, his school, noted for being innovative, was thriving. Valuing the importance of "learning by doing," he took the children on many excursions, during which he shared his knowledge of natural history, pointing out the details of plant, bird, and animal life.

On one particular occasion, Thoreau took a group of children down the Concord River. He pointed out a spot along the riverbank he thought might have been the site of an Indian fishing village and asked the students if they noticed anything there that would have made it well suited for that purpose. The students observed that it would have been ideal for fishing, that the nearby woods would have provided good hunting, and a spring would have supplied fresh drinking water. Thoreau pulled out a spade and began to dig along the shore; after several vain attempts, he finally uncovered an ancient Indian fireplace. Afterward, he covered the rocks over again so that someone else could discover them in the future.

Other field trips included visits to the *Yeoman's Gazette*, where the students could watch typesetters at work, and to the gunsmith shop, where they could watch the manufacture of gun sights. In the spring each student received a hoe and a little plot of land in which to sow seeds. To apply what they had learned about mathematics, Thoreau encouraged the students to try their hand at surveying the cliff at Fairhaven Bay.

Despite its success, the school lasted a little less than three years. John, suffering from tuberculosis, grew frail and thin as the disease progressed, and the physical demands of teaching became too much for him. Henry did not wish to continue teaching alone, and the school was closed on April 1, 1841.

With his life so full of disappointments and sorrows, Thoreau turned more and more to nature and his journal for comfort and inspiration.

"A Singular Character"

Thoreau was a confirmed bachelor by the mid-1840s, seizing every opportunity he could to deride both women and the institution of marriage. For instance, in his journal, Thoreau recorded a miserable evening he spent at a party:

> Was introduced to two young women. The first one was as lively and loquacious as a chickadee; had been accustomed to the society of watering-places, and therefore could get no refreshment out of such a dry fellow as I. The other was said to be pretty-looking, but I rarely look people in their faces, and moreover, I could not hear what she said, there was such a clacking ...
>
> The society of young women is the most unprofitable I have ever tried. They are so light and flighty that you can never be sure whether they are there or not there. I prefer to talk with the more staid and settled, settled for life, in every sense.

Not only did Thoreau avoid the company of young women, but he could also be as prudish as an old maid. He refused to listen to off-color jokes and coarse language. He had, after all, spent most of his life surrounded by bachelors and spinsters, including all his brothers and sisters, his five aunts, and uncles from both sides of his family, all of whom had lived at some time in the Thoreau household.

Shortly after Thoreau's return from his journey on the Merrimack in 1839, the members of the Transcendentalists' club, finding no periodicals willing to print what many considered heretical nonsense, decided to undertake the publication of a quarterly journal they called *The Dial* as a forum for their writings. The editor would be Margaret Fuller, one of the original members of the Hedge Club. Thoreau submitted the poem "Sympathy" for the first issue, which appeared in July of 1840. Emerson encouraged Thoreau to continue writing and submit poetry and essays, although Fuller did not always accept them.

In March of 1842, discouraged by the journal's low circulation and financial difficulties, Fuller relinquished the editorship. Since no one else was willing to undertake the job, Emerson took over as editor.

During her two years as editor, Margaret Fuller had only included four of Thoreau's poems and one translation, but with Emerson at the helm, this changed. In July of 1842, Thoreau's first major prose work was published, an essay called "The Natural History of Massachusetts," which was a review of several newly published natural history surveys issued by the Commonwealth of Massachusetts. The essay included excerpts from the best nature writings in Thoreau's journal.

His poetry was considered rough and irregular, even by Emerson, who wrote in his own journal: "Their fault is, that the gold does not yet flow pure, but is drossy and crude. The thyme and marjoram are not yet made into honey; the assimilation is imperfect." Thoreau was never a successful poet, but both his prose and his life itself were full of poetry. He wrote, "My life hath been the poem I would have writ, / But I could not both live and utter it."

Emerson asked Thoreau to do a translation of *Prometheus Unbound* for the January 1843 issue of *The Dial*. When Emerson's heavy lecture schedule prevented him from editing the April 1843 issue, Thoreau edited it by himself. He submitted translations from Pindar and an essay on Nathaniel P. Roger's antislavery weekly, *Herald of Freedom*, for the April 1844 issue, which would be *The Dial*'s last. Its circulation had never risen over one thousand, with subscriptions never reaching beyond three hundred. As a result, the staff had not been able to compensate its contributors and had difficulty paying the printing bills.

Although the journal was short-lived, it had provided a forum for the Transcendentalists and given several men and women their first chance to write professionally. Altogether, thirty-one of Thoreau's poems, essays, and translations had appeared in *The Dial*'s sixteen issues, giving him the exposure and confidence he needed.

With the journal's demise came the dissolution of the Transcendentalists as a group. The older members now pursued successful careers, while the younger ones, including Thoreau, were still so dedicated to Transcendentalism that they had no interest in pursuing a formal organization. Instead, they drew their inspiration from their own solitary musings.

After Thoreau's school closed, he sought a teaching position in Boston at the Perkins Institute for the Blind. When this attempt also failed, he abandoned any further hopes of teaching and instead turned his attention to finding a remote spot where he could devote his time to writing. He looked into several locations, hoping to find or rent a run-down farm, or some land where he could build a cabin. At one point he had arranged to purchase an old farm about two miles southwest of Concord Village, but the owner's wife changed her mind. His December 24 journal entry read:

> I want to go soon and live away by the pond, where I shall hear only the wind whispering among the reeds. It will be success if I shall have left myself behind. But my friends ask what I will do when I get there. Will it not be employment enough to watch the progress of the seasons?

Thoreau became increasingly restless while deciding what to do with his life and where he should set up residence.

A group of artists led by George Ripley, a friend of Emerson's, was struggling with the same issue. They decided that they should band together to form a commune where each person's energy and resources were pooled, minimizing the amount of time required to meet their physical needs, and leaving more time for their creative work. Ripley purchased some land in West Roxbury, a suburb of Boston, to create the Brook Farm Community.

On Prospect Hill in Harvard, Massachusetts, Bronson Alcott established a similar "community experiment" called Fruitlands, which embraced even more radical and eccentric values than Ripley's: members refused to eat meat of any kind, to use oxen to pull their plows, or to use animal manure to fertilize their gardens. They also wore only linen, avoiding cotton because of their opposition to slave labor.

Thoreau was invited to join both of these communities, but he had misgivings. His journal reads:

> As for these communities, I think I had rather keep bachelor's hall in hell than go to board in heaven. Do you think your virtue will be boarded with you? It will never live on the interest of your money, depend upon it. The boarder has no home. In heaven I hope to bake my own bread and clean my own linen. The tomb is the only boarding-house in which a hundred are served at once. In the catacomb we may dwell together and prop one another without loss.

Thoreau was too much an individualist to believe that life's problems could be solved in a community. He went his solitary way and believed firmly that reform always began with the individual, that the only person he could change was himself, not others. He never joined any of the many community experiments of his day. Apparently, he never even visited nearby Brook Farm, although many of his friends lived there.

Thoreau did find a temporary home with Emerson on Lexington Road in Concord, where he moved in April of 1841. This proved to be to their mutual benefit, since Emerson had never had much domestic or practical ability, while Thoreau was very handy at making repairs and gardening, tasks he performed for a couple of hours each day in return for his room and board.

With his own physical needs provided for, Thoreau was free to pursue his writing. He also had unlimited access to Emerson's library, from which he read voraciously. Emerson's books on Eastern philosophy, including *Heetopades of Veeshnoo-Sarma* and the *Laws of Menu,* especially interested Thoreau. He found their emphasis on solitude and contemplation, rather than the materialism of the Western culture in which he felt so out of place, more in line with his own philosophy of life.

Sharing a home enriched the friendship between Thoreau and Emerson, drawing them closer and replacing their pupil-mentor relationship with one of equality. Thoreau was often not easy to live with. He was sometimes easily offended, and refused to relent on the smallest, most trivial issues, declaring them matters of principle.

A friendship that was briefly important to Thoreau was that of Richard Fuller, Margaret's younger brother. After working in business for a time, Richard decided to attend Harvard, and Margaret thought that Thoreau would be an ideal tutor, someone who could assist her brother in accelerating his studies.

Richard Fuller came to Concord in the fall of 1841 and spent fourteen hours a day studying with Thoreau, resulting in Fuller's acceptance into Harvard as a sophomore the following February. In the process the two became good friends, and in mid-July they decided to take a four-day walk to Wachusett Mountain. They reached the summit of the mountain on the second day and pitched a tent, where they spent the night. The following day they descended the mountain and walked through Swiftwater, Sterling, Lancaster, and Still River until they reached the village of Harvard, where they spent the third night. They said good-bye to each other the following morning before walking on to their separate homes. Thoreau took notes during this excursion and worked them into an essay entitled "A Walk to Wachusett." He submitted it to the *Boston Miscellany of Literature*, and it was published in the January 1843 issue.

In January of 1842, while Thoreau was still living with the Emersons, he learned that his brother John had grown very ill after slicing a small piece of flesh from the tip of his left ring finger while stropping his razor. Within a few days of the accident, he was experiencing strange sensations and sharp pain; these symptoms were eventually followed by lockjaw. Already weakened by tuberculosis, John's condition quickly grew serious. Henry returned home to nurse John and stayed at his bedside until his brother died in his arms on January 11. John's death had a profound effect on Henry; shortly afterward he suffered from a psychosomatic illness that produced symptoms very similar to John's.

Within a couple of weeks, Emerson was struck with his own tragedy when his five-year-old son Waldo became ill with scarlet fever and died. Their mutual grief drew Emerson and Thoreau even closer. Thoreau had moved back to his parents' home at the time of his brother's death, but he soon returned to the Emersons'.

In July of 1842, Thoreau struck up a new acquaintance with Nathaniel Hawthorne when Hawthorne and his wife came to live in Concord. Hawthorne had this to say about Thoreau:

> He is a singular character—a young man with much of wild original nature still remaining in him; and so far as he is sophisticated it is in a way and method of his own ... Mr. Thorow [sic] is a keen and delicate observer of nature—a genuine observer, which, I suspect, is almost as rare a character as even an original poet; and Nature, in return for his love, seems to adopt him as her especial child, and shows him secrets which few others are allowed to witness.

Hawthorne appreciated Thoreau's unpretentiousness, and the two men spent many hours rowing together on the Concord River. Upon reading Thoreau's essay, "Natural History of Massachusetts," Hawthorne wrote: "[it] gives a very fair image of his mind and character—so true, minute, and literal in observation, yet giving the spirit as well as letter of what he sees, even as a lake reflects its wooded banks ..."

Hawthorne also went out of his way to further Thoreau's writing career by mentioning him in the prefaces of his books *Mosses from an Old Manse* and *The Scarlet Letter*, as well as pointing out his talents to the editors of *New Monthly Magazine* and *Democratic Review*. J.L. O'Sullivan, the editor of the latter, asked Thoreau to write something for his magazine. When Thoreau obliged with a review of J.A. Etzler's *The Paradise Within the Reach of All Men*, O'Sullivan asked him to instead submit some excerpts from his journal containing his many observations of nature.

Etzler's book was a Utopian piece which suggested that if human beings were only to utilize the sources of energy available to them, chiefly the sun, winds, and tides, and put into effect mass-production methods, they would eliminate the need for real labor and would be able to live in a kind of paradise. Etzler's ideas seemed fanciful and unrealistic to some nineteenth-century readers, but in fact he foresaw many real inventions.

O'Sullivan was worried that Thoreau would offend some *Democratic Review* readers with his review of the book, since Thoreau took issue with Etzler's positions. So the two arrived at a compromise in which Thoreau agreed to bring his views a little more in line with the editor's. The result was Thoreau's "Paradise (to be) Regained," which was published in the November 1843 issue. Thoreau remained true to his Transcendentalist principles, however, stating: "We believe that most things will have to be accomplished still by the application called Industry." He also stressed that human love is the most powerful energy of all. "It can make a paradise within which will dispense with a paradise without."

By the spring of 1843, Thoreau had been living with the Emersons for about two years, and he again began to feel restless.

Ellyn Sanna

FOLLOWING HIS DREAMS

Emerson visited his brother William on Staten Island that spring and assisted in securing employment for Thoreau as tutor to William's son Willie. Emerson was hopeful that close proximity to New York City would also aid Thoreau with his writing career. A salary of $100 a year was settled upon, which included board and lodging, as well as a room with a fire where Thoreau could study in the evenings. He left for Staten Island on May 6, 1843.

Thoreau taught from 9 A.M. to 2 P.M. and often took Willie and a neighbor boy from across the street on walks or fishing early in the morning before lessons. As usual, the time he found most enjoyable was that which he spent by himself when he took off to explore the island, with all its new and unusual flora and fauna. What he found most exciting was the sea; he would sit by the hour watching ships sail up the coast.

By contrast, he found the city a disappointment:

> I don't like the city better, the more I see it, but worse. I am ashamed of my eyes that behold it. It is a thousand times meaner than I could have imagined. It will be something to hate—that's the advantage it will be to me; and even the best people in it are a part of it and talk coolly about it. The pigs in the street are the most respectable part of the population. When will the world learn that a million men are of no importance compared with *one* man?

There were a few bright spots during his stay in New York, among them his meeting with the father of novelist Henry James. Thoreau also renewed his acquaintance with Horace Greeley, the editor of the New York *Tribune*, whom he had met at the Concord Lyceum the year before. Greeley acted as Thoreau's literary agent and had some of Thoreau's essays published in the best periodicals of the day, as well as in his own paper.

Another advantage of living in New York was the availability of books and libraries. Thoreau discovered that one of his tutors at Harvard, H.S. McKean, was in charge of the Mercantile Library, and through him Thoreau was able to obtain visitor's cards permitting him to take out books.

Thoreau's hopes of finding a publisher did not materialize—although he made a connection with Harper's and a few other publishers, they were unwilling to take a chance on a new and unknown author, especially when they were already saturated with contributions.

Thoreau became unbearably lonely and unhappy while living with William Emerson's family in New York. His health suffered, presumably from the moist climate that aggravated his tuberculosis; he was homesick for Concord, his family, and the Emersons, as his letters home showed clearly; and he was terribly grieved when he received word that his old friend Stearns Wheeler, with whom he had attended college, had died. But perhaps the most important reason for his unhappiness was that he found no sense of kinship with his employers. William Emerson was too conservative for Thoreau, and Thoreau was too much of an individualist for his host.

Thoreau decided he would visit home over Thanksgiving, since Ralph Emerson had asked him to lecture at the Lyceum if he returned. Thoreau intended to stay in Concord only a short time, but once home he knew he would be unable to go back to New York, except to fetch his possessions, which he did on December 3. He settled back into his old life, living again on Main Street with his family.

He needed money to pay off his debts, so he returned to work in the pencil factory. Looking at the procedure with a new eye after having been away from it for some time, Thoreau quickly developed new techniques. He developed a saw that stripped the baked lead so it would fit into the grooved pencil halves, then improved the process even further when he came up with the idea of baking the graphite in cylinders the exact size needed for the pencils, thus eliminating the step of sawing out the individual leads. Finally, he invented a machine that drilled holes through the lengths of the pencils so the leads could be fed into them, rather than splitting the pencil wood in half and gluing the halves back together again—a painstaking process. He also discovered that he could create varying degrees of hardness in the leads by adding or decreasing the amounts of clay in the formula. These high-quality pencils were the best on the market, suitable for artists and engineers. Henry's efforts made the family business even more successful and earned the Thoreaus recognition; they won a diploma at the annual fair in 1847, as well as the silver medal for the best lead pencils at the Salem Charitable Mechanic Association in 1849.

About this time, Thoreau developed another important friendship with George William Curtis, the son of a Providence businessman; he and his brother Burrill spent some time with the Brook Farm Community, and then they went to Concord, drawn there by Emerson. They rented rooms from a farmer named Barrett and pursued an existence very similar to Thoreau's, laboring on the farm for half the day and boating, talking, walking, and writing for the rest. In later years, Curtis would became the editor of *Putnam's* and be helpful to Thoreau's literary career.

Ellery Channing, whom Thoreau met in 1840 at Emerson's home, would become the most intimate and lasting friend of Thoreau's life. Overindulged and spoiled as a child, Channing had attended Harvard briefly, then dropped out to live alone for a time in a cabin on the Illinois prairie. Channing often met Thoreau when he returned to Concord for visits; by 1842, he was married to Margaret Fuller's sister Ellen and when he decided to settle in Concord in 1843, Thoreau helped the couple find a house to rent, then undertook the necessary home repairs as a favor to Channing. In return, Channing offered to let Thoreau live with them, but by then he had made arrangements to go to Staten Island. They continued their friendship when Thoreau returned, but by April of 1844, Channing had accepted a job on Horace Greeley's *Tribune*.

The two men made plans to take an excursion together in mid-summer and arranged to meet at Saddleback Mountain in northwestern Massachusetts. They traveled to the Hudson, where they boated downriver to the Catskills to hike. Channing was to look upon his relationship with Thoreau as "*the* great event of his life," and he was the first to publish a biography of Thoreau after his death. Channing described Thoreau's mannerisms with the insight of a close friend:

> His whole figure had an active earnestness, as if he had no moment to waste. The clenched hand betokened purpose. In walking, he made a short cut if he could, and when sitting in the shade or by the wallside seemed merely the clearer to look forward into the next piece of activity. Even in the boat he had a wary, transitory air, his eyes on the outlook— perhaps there might be ducks, or the blondin turtle, or an otter, or sparrow.

On August 1, 1844, the women's antislavery organization in Concord persuaded Emerson to deliver a speech commemorating the anniversary of the emancipation of the slaves in the British West Indies. Prior to this time, he had been reluctant to give voice to his opinions on the subject, even though most everyone knew he was sympathetic to the abolitionist cause. The women's group had urged the public to attend the meeting in the courthouse hall, but the sexton of the First Parish Church, who would normally have announced the meeting by ringing the town bell in the church steeple, refused to do so. No one would step forward to ring the bell, since the abolitionist movement was still so controversial in Concord. When Thoreau heard of the problem, he rushed to the church and rang the bell vigorously, gathering a large crowd to hear the speech.

One of the members of the Concord organization, Anna Maria Whiting, recorded the events of the meeting and sent a report to the *Herald of Freedom*, where it was published by Nathaniel Rogers in September. Later, Thoreau negotiated on the antislavery group's behalf to have Emerson's address printed in pamphlet form by James Munroe & Company of Boston.

The members of the Concord Lyceum disagreed regarding abolitionism, and the opposing factions were unable to come to a consensus. In December of 1842, Thoreau invited Wendell Phillips to speak, in the face of violent opposition from the Lyceum's conservative members. Each time Phillips was invited to speak, the same argument erupted, but the conservatives were always outvoted. In his speeches, Phillips destroyed each of the dissenters' arguments.

Finally, in the spring of 1845, the conservative curators of the Lyceum resigned and were replaced by Emerson, Thoreau, and Samuel Barrett. Thoreau sent a letter to William Lloyd Garrison, the editor of the antislavery *Liberator*, defending Phillips's right to speak. Freedom of speech in the Concord Lyceum had finally been guaranteed.

Meanwhile, because of Thoreau's contributions to the pencil factory, the business was thriving, and his mother decided that the family could now afford to build a house rather than rent, as they had always done. Thoreau was more than willing to do his share and curtailed his time spent in the woods to work longer hours in the factory. He had often been accused of freeloading off his family; conscious of that perception, he took pains to pay rent to his father faithfully throughout his adult life. When a lot was purchased for the new home on Texas Street (the house would be called the Texas House), Henry dug the cellar and laid the stones by himself before he and his father undertook the rest of the construction.

Busy with friendships, the Lyceum, and his family responsibilities, Thoreau was often distracted from his writing goals. Years had passed since the trip he and John had taken down the Merrimack and Concord Rivers in 1839, and he still had not begun working on the book he intended to write about the experience. He needed a writing retreat, somewhere away from life's distractions, where he could go to concentrate only on writing. With Emerson's help, he moved to Walden Pond.

Once there, one of the first writing assignments he completed was an essay on the works of Thomas Carlyle. He presented it as a lecture before the Concord Lyceum in February of 1846, but he soon discovered that his listeners were more interested in learning his reasons for leaving the conventional world for a life in the woods. They wanted to know if he felt lonely and afraid by himself in the woods; they wondered what he ate, and if he gave his money away to charity. These questions prompted him to write a series of lectures about his life that were eventually compiled into his great work, *Walden, or Life in the Woods*. When he delivered the first of these lectures about his life a year later, the reaction from the townspeople was so favorable, he was asked to repeat it the next week for any who had missed it.

By July of 1846, Thoreau had finally completed the first draft of his account of the voyage down the Concord and Merrimack Rivers. Emerson tried to convince him to send it to a publisher right away, but Thoreau felt it needed revising.

Emerson visited Thoreau at the cabin and even made out a new will, leaving Thoreau the land on which his cabin was built. Meanwhile, Thoreau continued to take care of any odd jobs that needed doing around the Emerson home, even performing some surveying for him. Other visitors at Walden Pond included shy Nathaniel Hawthorne, who considered Walden a haven, and Bronson Alcott, who brought his family and other guests from time to time.

Despite the visitors, Thoreau never lost sight of his real purpose for living on Walden Pond. He had come there primarily for a period of solitude, and to commune with nature; he considered watching the loons and geese on the pond or the foxes and hawks in the woods, even the ants in the grass or the clouds overhead, an occupation so essential to his being that it was akin to religious devotion. Through nature, Thoreau touched the transcendental reality in which he believed.

By 1847, after he had been at Walden two years, he again began to feel restless. He had accomplished the writing he had set out to do and more, completing not only the excursion book but *Walden* as well. Deciding that his experiment at Walden had served its purpose, he accepted an invitation from Emerson, who would be lecturing abroad, to join his family for the winter so that they would not be alone.

Thoreau always felt that living at Walden had been one of the high points of his life. He wrote: "I learned this, at least, by my experiment; that if one advances confidently in the direction of his dreams, and endeavors to live the life which he has imagined, he will meet with a success unexpected in common hours."

While in England, Emerson did his best to promote Thoreau's literary talent, forecasting that his friend would one day be famous. In 1855, in the biography he wrote of Emerson, George Searle Phillips made sure to properly emphasize his friendship with Thoreau.

CIVIL DISOBEDIENCE

Thoreau's first act of civil disobedience actually began in 1840, concerning the matter of a church tax bill. Because his family had always attended the First Parish Church where they owned a pew, and Thoreau himself had attended as a child, church officials automatically added his name to the tax rolls. When he received his first tax bill, he visited the town office and refused to pay. The town officers threatened to send him to jail, but before this could happen, someone anonymously paid the tax for him.

Knowing that he would have to contend with the issue again in the future, Thoreau filed a statement with the town selectmen (board of officials), stating: "Know all men by these present, that I, Henry Thoreau, do not wish to be regarded as a member of any incorporated society which I have not joined." He asked them for a list of any other incorporated societies to whose membership he might have been added without his knowledge, and at that they were willing to let the matter drop; he never again received a bill for church taxes.

In late July 1846, Thoreau once more felt impelled to follow his conscience when, while in town to pick up a shoe from the cobbler's, he was approached by the local constable, who asked him to pay his poll tax for the last several years. Thoreau had resisted paying this tax previously as a matter of conscience; he felt that a country built upon democratic principles should not allow slavery. Mr. Staples, the constable, bore Thoreau no animosity; in fact, he offered to pay the tax for Thoreau himself if Thoreau had no money and suggested that he appeal to the selectmen to reduce the tax. Thoreau explained that principle rather than lack of money had prompted his refusal to pay. When Staples asked what he should do about it, Thoreau replied that he could resign if he didn't like it.

"Henry," Staples was forced to reply, "if you don't pay, I shall have to lock you up pretty soon."

"As well now as any time, Sam," Thoreau answered.

"Well, come along then," Staples said, perhaps with a sigh.

After Thoreau was taken to jail, a heavily veiled person passed a package through the door, saying, "Here is the money to pay Mr. Thoreau's tax." Some historians have speculated that Emerson or one of Thoreau's aunts paid the tax—his Aunt Maria once admitted to an old family friend that she was the benefactor.

Thoreau was not happy about being rescued from jail; in fact, he was very angry that his arrest, which he'd hoped would call the attention of his fellow citizens to the antislavery cause, had been thwarted. Since he himself had not paid the taxes, he felt he had the right to stay in jail. But Staples said, "Henry, if you will not go of your own accord I shall put you out, for you cannot stay here any longer."

Many of Thoreau's fellow townspeople disapproved of his actions. Even Emerson was disgusted with him; he told Alcott that what Thoreau had done was "mean and sulking, and in bad taste." The next time Emerson saw Thoreau, he asked him why he had gone to jail, to which Thoreau replied "Why did you not?"

Each year thereafter, someone continued to anonymously pay Thoreau's tax in advance. Even so, many townspeople were curious about Thoreau's reasons for wanting to go to jail. In response, Thoreau presented an explanation as a two-part lecture at the Concord Lyceum in the winter of 1848. Later, in the spring of 1849, Elizabeth Peabody asked Thoreau's permission to publish the lecture in a new periodical she had begun called the *Aesthetic Papers*. The lecture was printed in the first and only issue in May of 1849, along with essays by Emerson and Hawthorne, which received much more notice than did Thoreau's "Resistance to Civil Government" (as it was called before becoming "Civil Disobedience" in 1866, after Thoreau's death).

Although it received little attention at the time, "Civil Disobedience" is probably Thoreau's most powerful and influential political essay, one in which he expressed his belief that the law of conscience is a higher law than civil law—and that when these laws are in conflict, it is the citizen's duty to obey the voice of God within rather than that of civil authority. If a person will go to prison rather than obey an evil law, Thoreau said, he will rouse the conscience of other people, who will in turn be inspired to change the government. Mahatma Gandhi and Martin Luther King Jr. exemplified Thoreau's principles put to action.

In the midst of his civil efforts, Thoreau continued to write. Remembering an offer of help from Horace Greeley of the New York *Tribune*, in mid-summer of 1846 Thoreau sent off the essay he had prepared on Carlyle, hoping that Greeley would be able to find a publisher for it. *Graham's Magazine* agreed to publish it, but it was a trying experience for Thoreau—the essay finally appeared in print in March of the following year, but it wasn't until March of 1848 that he received payment for it, and then only with Greeley's help.

The work on Carlyle was the only "piece of extended literary criticism" that Thoreau ever produced. He was so soured by his experience with the literary magazine that he wanted nothing to do with the efforts of Emerson and several of his friends, including Theodore Parker, Bronson Alcott, and George Bradford, to establish the *Massachusetts Quarterly Review* (which produced only three volumes). Nor did he want any part in Emerson's wish to establish a transatlantic magazine. When Emerson suggested Thoreau could write for the publication, Thoreau answered that he was "more interested in the private journal than the public one."

In March of 1848, Thoreau shared an account of life at Walden Pond with Greeley, who published it in his New York *Tribune* for May 25, 1948, with his own introductory editorial. Greeley also included a portion of a personal letter Thoreau had written to him, and begged Thoreau to not be angry with him for including part of his letter; he felt the inclusion would do great good for promotion of *Walden*. Pleased rather than angered by the inclusion, Thoreau decided to include the quotes in his first chapter of *Walden*.

Thoreau continued to have rewarding relationships with male friends, but no further romantic pursuits ever were recorded—though he was apparently the object of the unwanted affections of Sophia Ford, a woman fifteen years his senior. In November of 1847, while Emerson was still abroad, Thoreau wrote to tell his friend he had received an unwelcome proposal of marriage from Miss Ford.

A Transcendentalist and an abolitionist herself, Ford had spent some time at a community experiment in Massachusetts similar to Brook Farm, and she had become acquainted with Bronson Alcott, who hired her as a teacher. She added the Channing and Emerson children as pupils later, but left Concord for a time when she became ill. In March of 1847 she left permanently. She and Thoreau corresponded for a while; her proposal to him came in a letter six months after her departure. When he refused, it was rumored that Ford was so heartbroken, she threatened to commit suicide. Years later, she told an employer in Rhode Island, where she worked as a governess, "that Thoreau's soul was a twin to hers and that in 'the other world' her spirit and his would be united." Thoreau felt no such kinship.

SUCCESSES AND SETBACKS

In the summer of 1846, Thoreau accompanied his cousin George Thatcher from Bangor, Maine, on an excursion to Mount Katahdin. On January 5, 1848, he delivered a lecture on the subject at the Concord Lyceum, and since it was well received, he decided to submit it for publication in the *Tribune*. Greeley paid him $25 for the piece, but felt the article was "too fine for the million"; instead of publishing it in his newspaper, he placed it instead in *Sartain's Union Magazine*, where it was presented in five installments. When Emerson read the essay, he decided it was the first piece of American literature he had seen in ten years that was worth binding.

Although Greeley had publicly issued his approval of Thoreau's Katahdin essay, privately he warned Thoreau that if he wished to be published in the periodicals, he should write shorter pieces. Greeley suggested specifically that Thoreau write an essay on the literary life.

Thoreau had a tendency to become stubborn whenever anyone suggested he *should* do something, and informed Greeley that he was too busy writing his books. Greeley replied that Thoreau would facilitate his career if he could be published in periodicals; he could wait to write books. When Thoreau again refused, Greeley suggested that Thoreau send along some passages from his books for advance publication. Still annoyed, Thoreau delayed accepting even that invitation for quite some time.

Although Thoreau did not always cooperate with the men who sought to mentor him, he too began to mentor others who came to him for inspiration and direction. His first and one of his most devoted disciples was Gray Otis Blake of Worcester, Massachusetts, whom Thoreau had known at least superficially since Harvard, where Blake had attended the divinity school, two years ahead of Thoreau. He had been the pastor of a church in Milford, New Hampshire, for a time, but began to question church dogma after hearing Emerson's "Divinity School Address" and left to teach school, eventually ending up in Worcester. He was a frequent visitor at Emerson's home, where he and Thoreau met occasionally.

Blake stumbled upon an old copy of *The Dial* that contained one of Thoreau's essays. Convinced of Thoreau's genuine genius, Blake sat down and wrote him a letter. The two men began a correspondence, with Thoreau writing some of the longest and most philosophical letters of his life, numbering at least forty-nine.

Whenever he received a letter from Thoreau, Blake invited a circle of friends to listen to selected passages from the letter. He so valued Thoreau's letters, he thought of editing them for publication. Blake regularly invited Thoreau to lecture in Worcester, and often visited him in Concord. During these years when Thoreau received no recognition from the world at large, Blake's admiration and respect must have been a comfort.

Emerson had returned from his trip abroad by late July of 1848, and Thoreau moved back to his parents' house. He returned to his occasional odd jobs, and spent some time working in the pencil factory. A fire at the steam mill in Concord where the wooden parts of their pencils were produced had left the Thoreau family with another financial loss—between $400 and $500 of the materials lost in the fire had been uninsured.

Thoreau soon became bored with factory work, and turned to surveying, a profession much more to his liking, and one that provided him with a good and fairly steady income. He also began to seek income on the lecture circuit, where he would be able to test out his writings in front of an audience before attempting to have them published, and create a market for the books he intended to publish at the same time.

The first audience Thoreau addressed outside of Concord was at the Salem Lyceum on November 22, 1848, arranged by his friend Nathaniel Hawthorne. His lecture was called "Student Life in New England, Its Economy," which was to be an early version of the "Economy" chapter of *Walden*. The review printed in the *Salem Observer* was quite favorable, stating that while the lecture was "sufficiently *Emersonian* to have come from the great philosopher himself," it "furnished ample proof of being a native product, by affording all the charm of an original," with observations "sufficiently queer to keep the audience in almost constant mirth, and sufficiently wise and new to afford many good practical hints and precepts." The performance, the reviewer concluded, had "created quite a sensation."

Thoreau gave the lecture again in Gloucester, though not with as much success, and then went on to Portland, Maine, where the lecture was enjoyed immensely, described as "unique, original, comical, and high-falutin."

Thanks to his friend Blake, Thoreau lectured at Worcester more frequently than any other place besides Concord. Hearing of Thoreau's lecture tour, Horace Greeley decided to promote his lectures in an editorial in the *Tribune*, making Thoreau the source of much pride in his hometown.

In 1845, Wiley & Putnam were establishing a new series of "American Books" in an effort to overcome the predominance of English authors on the American book market. Evert Duyckink asked Nathaniel Hawthorne to write a volume and inquired about any promising new authors who might also be able to contribute. Hawthorne suggested Thoreau but warned:

> As for Thoreau, there is one chance in a thousand that he might write a most excellent and readable book; but I should be sorry to take the responsibility, either towards you or him, of stirring him up to write anything ... He is the most

unmalleable fellow alive—the most tedious, tiresome, and intolerable—the narrowest and most notional—and yet, true as all this is, he has great qualities of intellect and character.

Meanwhile, Thoreau had been working on the book commemorating his trip on the Concord and Merrimack Rivers with his brother John, but he did not have it revised to his satisfaction until March of 1847. When he was ready to submit it, Emerson wrote to Wiley & Putnam on Thoreau's behalf; the publisher accepted it for publication, but stipulated that Thoreau had to pay all the publishing costs. This, of course, was prohibitive for Thoreau, so he sent the book to a Boston publisher, James Munroe & Co., only to have them propose the same arrangement. After trying Harper's and Ticknor & Co. of Boston with no luck, he returned to James Munroe & Co., who offered to print *A Week on the Concord and Merrimack Rivers* and let Thoreau pay the costs out of sales, so long as he guaranteed that they would eventually receive the full amount. Once *A Week on the Concord and Merrimack Rivers* was published, they would follow it with *Walden*.

This agreement worried Thoreau's aunts and sisters a good deal. They were afraid the book would never sell well enough to enable Thoreau to reimburse the publishers.

The book was officially published on May 30, 1849, with very little advance publicity. The book narrated the actual voyage, describing what they saw, where they camped, and some of the history of the area they were passing through, with one chapter for each day of the journey; this straightforward narration constituted a little less than half of the book, and might have made for a popular piece of easy reading.

The rest of the book had little connection with the travel narrative. It was a collection of essays, poems, translations, and quotations, all collected together into the narrative with little rhyme or reason. Many of these digressions were taken from Thoreau's contributions to *The Dial*—poems, translations, remarks on Chaucer—and a few were lecture notes he had never managed to get into print before. Most of these were good writing in and of themselves, but they did not belong in the middle of the narrative of a voyage on the Concord and Merrimack Rivers. What's more, Thoreau's comments on religion antagonized the more conservative readers of his day.

The book received mixed reviews. Surprisingly, an English

journal, the *Athenaeum* of October 27, 1849, gave Thoreau one of the most favorable reviews, commenting:

> The matter is for the most part poor enough; but there are a few things in the volume scattered here and there, which suggest that the writer is a man with a habit of original thinking which with more careful culture may produce a richer harvest in some future season.

Reviews aside, the book was not a success. Out of 1,000 copies printed, the sellers returned 706 to the publisher, leaving Thoreau with a very heavy debt. It took him four years to repay it, and since the publisher needed the room, Thoreau had the leftover 706 copies sent to his home. He observed: "I have now a library of nearly nine hundred volumes, over seven hundred of which I wrote myself." It had cost him $290 to publish his book; his total income from the book was only $15. As a result, Munroe & Co. would not publish *Walden*, and Thoreau was unable to interest anyone else until years later.

Thoreau's family affairs were troubling as well. In the winter of 1849, his sister Helen's health rapidly declined, as she suffered more severely from her tuberculosis. Letters from his Aunt Maria to Prudence Ward show Helen had reconciled herself to the fact that she was dying: "She says she has not a gloomy thought about it, and she would not if she could come back again to life to suffer what she had done with ill health ..." According to Maria, Helen did not feel that her funeral should be a sad occasion. She died on June 14, 1849, at the age of thirty-six. As a tribute to her, Thoreau wrote a poem called "Farewell," one of the very few he wrote in his later years.

Despite this tragedy, the family was prospering financially. Their business underwent a transformation during the late 1840s to early 1850s due to a sudden increase in demand for lead from the Boston firm of Smith & McDougal. The huge demand mystified the Thoreaus, who wondered if Smith & McDougal planned to go into the pencil business themselves. After pledging the Thoreaus to secrecy, the firm admitted that the high quality of the Thoreaus' lead made it particularly suitable for use in the newly invented electrotyping process.

In order to keep Smith & McDougal's business and avoid competition, the Thoreaus kept this fact a secret and began making the lead from their home, using the manufacture of pencils as a cover-up for their real activity. Eventually their secret leaked out, and competitors slowly drove the price down from the $10 a pound the Thoreaus had been earning to $2 a pound, but the Thoreaus were still able to make a very good living.

This new prosperity, combined with Mrs. Thoreau's wishes, allowed the Thoreaus to move closer to town, into a finer house on Main Street. The house was raised to accommodate higher ceilings, a mahogany staircase and fireplaces were added, and the barn was attached to the house to create a place for the family business. Two young girls were also hired to assist with housekeeping.

Thoreau was initially reluctant to move to this new residence, but later he had to admit his room—the finished attic in the main portion of the house, with an open stairway in the center of the room, sloping ceilings, and windows at both ends—was much more pleasant and convenient than any he'd ever had before. He furnished the room with bookshelves he made from driftwood boards he had gathered along the river, and later added nooks where he displayed things he had found during his ramblings in the woods—curious rocks, lichens and mosses, and old books filled with preserved flowers. He kept his collection of birds' eggs and Native American artifacts in a bureau, and filled one bookcase with his journal; deer antlers he had picked up in Maine and snowshoes he had purchased from the Indians adorned the walls. His only other furniture was the cot he had slept in at Walden, a bureau, and two chairs. Here, in the cozy and idiosyncratic hideout he had created, he could read and write in undisturbed peace.

Thoreau continued to value his solitude but, as always, he also had his social side. He spent part of each evening with his family, and enjoyed listening to his sister play the piano; he often joined in the singing. He settled into a comfortable way of living, balancing solitude and companionship, enjoying solitary moments alone with nature while also studying and discussing the thoughts and knowledge of others. Although he still had not achieved any great fame as an author, his mind was not static. Rooted safely in Concord, he continued to grow and to explore the world around him.

Physical and Intellectual Adventures

Even at this late stage of his life, Thoreau continued his studies. He had lifetime use of the college library at Harvard, but not without exercising a little ingenuity to obtain this access. Ordinarily, only Cambridge residents were allowed to borrow books; Thoreau, having been denied the privilege by the librarian, went straight to the president of the college. The president eventually gave in to Thoreau's arguments, but by 1845, he had retired, and was replaced by Jared Sparks.

When Thoreau visited the library again, Sparks told him that only resident graduates, clergymen who were members of the alumni, or residents living within a ten-mile radius of the college were allowed to take out books. Thoreau replied that the railroad made the ten-mile radius an obsolete figure—he could now reach Cambridge quite quickly by train from Concord. When he explained that his need for books was far greater now than it had ever been in his college days, Sparks also gave in, but specified "one year" as Thoreau's term for using the library at the bottom of his letter of permission. Thoreau ignored this specification and continued to use the library for the rest of his life. He rarely visited Boston or Cambridge without taking out a book or two from the library.

He also gained access to the Boston Society of Natural History. In 1849 a friend of Thoreau's caught an American goshawk from the north and brought it for him to inspect, knowing his interest in such things. Thoreau, realizing how rare the bird was, took it to the Boston Society of Natural History, where the curator dissected, stuffed, and preserved it. A year later Thoreau was elected by the society to become an honorary corresponding member, which automatically gave him access to the library. Thereafter, he made many visits to the society, consulting with the curators and withdrawing books whenever he visited Boston. In return, Thoreau sent them copies of his books, as well as several of his essays.

Thoreau's love of nature and adventure did not abate as he grew older. On October 9, 1849, he and his friend Ellery Channing made an excursion to Cape Cod, where they hiked around Nauset Harbor, across Jeremiah's Gutter to Eastham, and then to Nauset Lights, discovering jellyfish, shells, driftwood, and fragments of old wrecks as they walked along the Back Side shore. They stayed the night with an old Wellfleet oysterman and his wife, who spent hours sharing the lore of the Cape and the sea with them. The next day they headed northward until they reached Highland Light, where they toured the lighthouse with the light-keeper as he lit the lamps. They continued along the shore the following day and climbed Mount Ararat, one of the largest of the sand dunes.

Upon arriving home, Thoreau read every book he could find about Cape Cod and then prepared a lecture about his adventure to share with the Concord Lyceum on January 23 and 30, 1850. Emerson later reported that the lecture was a huge success and people in the audience "laughed until they cried." In June of 1850, Thoreau returned to Cape Cod by himself to gather more writing material.

While Thoreau continued to pursue his interests, he was also hired frequently for his surveying services. By December of 1850 he had noted more than twenty completed surveys in his survey book, including the survey for the new courthouse and townhouse lots. He was even busier the following year. The task he found the most interesting was perambulating the town boundaries with the selectmen, during which he discovered that discrepancies had occurred over the years because of variations in compasses. He enjoyed the challenge of straightening out the boundaries, but he was irked by having to constantly rub shoulders with the town selectmen. Their trivial concerns made him feel "inexpressibly begrimed," as though he were destroying an essential part of his being. For days after the task was over, he wandered alone in the fields, trying to recover his "tone and sanity," trying "to perceive things truly and simply again."

Surveying provided him with a small but adequate income while bringing him to new fields and woods where he occasionally discovered flowers, birds, and mushrooms he had never seen before. Once in a while, he even found Indian relics. He also enjoyed running into colorful individuals who could tell him long stories about the history of Concord. These aspects of the work energized the artistic and creative side of his nature, even though the labor of surveying tired him physically.

Thoreau wondered if he was often too busy surveying to do what he really loved. On December 14, 1851, he discovered that boys had been skating for a week, and he had not only failed to put his skates on, but he had been so busy surveying he had hardly been aware that there was ice. According to his journal, he would have needed to earn a considerable amount of money to make up for the loss of a week's skating.

Still full of the spirit of adventure, in the early fall of 1850 Thoreau and Channing each paid $7 for a round trip to Canada by rail, and arrived in Montreal that afternoon, along with fifteen hundred other people. Visiting the Church of Notre Dame, Thoreau was impressed with the beautiful and quiet building, admitting in his journal that "the Catholic religion might be an admirable one—if only the priests were omitted." He also objected to the ever-present show of military might. Everywhere he looked there were soldiers, which Thoreau considered a waste of time, money, and energy.

From Montreal, they took a steamer to Quebec City and then hiked eight miles to Montmorency Falls—a disappointment, since a huge estate built by Queen Victoria's father fenced off the areas that afforded the best views. This time, Thoreau's journal entry was full of complaints about people who were selfish enough to restrict others from viewing the beauties of nature.

The two men continued walking along the St. Lawrence until they reached St. Anne, thirty miles downstream. Here, they found the falls more rewarding. "Falls there are a drug," Thoreau confessed, "and we became quite dissipated in respect to them."

When Thoreau returned home, he read as many books as he could find on Canadian history, and then he wrote an essay on his journey, "A Yankee in Canada," which he submitted to Horace Greeley for publication. Greeley, fearing Thoreau would alienate readers, suggested that he remove the references to church and state, but Thoreau apparently did not listen to Greeley's advice; the essay was rejected by two magazines before it was finally accepted by *Putnam's Monthly* to be published in installments. Thoreau demanded that his manuscript be returned before it had been completely published when the editor insisted on removing his comment about omitting priests from Catholicism.

The article turned out to be the least successful of Thoreau's excursion essays. He himself concluded that he had picked the wrong area of Canada to visit; his journey had taken him only to the small part of the country that was then urbanized. What he should have visited, he realized, was the great Canadian wilderness. He closed his essay with the hope that someday he might "make a longer excursion on foot through the wilder parts of Canada"—a journey he never had the opportunity to make.

As busy as he was with travel and writing, Thoreau continued to be in demand for lecturing. In April 1851 he tried out a new lecture called "The Wild" at the Concord Lyceum. This became one of his favorite lectures, one he repeated many times, working it over and adding to it each time he delivered it, until eventually he had enough material to split it into two parts, titling the new part "Walking." Because he knew the market for his lectures would vanish once the material reached print, he was careful not to have either part published until eleven years later, when he put the two back together again and sold the essay to *Atlantic Monthly* for publication in the June 1862 issue as "Walking, or the Wild."

The essay is still actually two separate pieces; in the first section he says he cannot preserve his health and spirits without spending at least four hours a day "sauntering through the woods and over the hills and fields, absolutely free from all worldly engagements," and in the second section he expresses his belief that humanity must return to the soil if we are to preserve our sanity, our morality, and our strength. The essay is a plea to save some of the wildness of the earth for future generations; it is one of the earliest documents in the conservation and national park movement.

Even though Thoreau was involved in writing, lecturing, and surveying, he still devoted a great deal of time each day to walking the woods and fields of Concord and surrounding towns. He set out each afternoon, well prepared with an old music book in which to press flowers and a cane made of a gnarled stick, one side shaved smooth and its edge marked off in feet and inches for quick measuring. His hat had a special shelf built inside on which to place interesting botanical specimens—his brains, he confided to his journal, helped to keep the specimens moist. He chose clothes that provided him with camouflage in the woods and fields—Vermont gray or, when he could find it, a mixture of browns and greens that made him look, he said "the color of a pasture."

As time went on, Thoreau began to apply a more scientific approach to his nature studies. He kept longer and longer lists of the specimens he found and recorded the dates when trees budded, flowers blossomed, and birds arrived; he collected, dried, and labeled botanical specimens. Eventually, he was able to locate more than eight hundred of the twelve hundred known species of Middlesex County.

In July of 1851, he visited a resident of Concord who had built a homemade telescope, which prompted him to make another visit to Cambridge to read up on astronomy. In spite of his fascination with the subject, he, like many of his contemporaries, feared that "science was destroying the beauty, the poetry of life." He sensed a change in himself that he was not comfortable with:

> I fear that the character of my knowledge is from year to year becoming more distinct and scientific; that in exchange for views as wide as heaven's scope, I am being narrowed down to the field of the microscope. I see details, not wholes nor the shadow of the whole. I count some parts, and say "I know."

Whatever his private fears, as time went on Thoreau's neighbors began to appreciate his expertise and authority when it came to the natural world around them, and they would bring him Native American relics, flowers, or birds' nests they could not identify. When he knew the answers to their questions he was happy to share them, and if he did not know the answers he would investigate them, but, as he confided to his journal, he could not allow his neighbors to intrude upon the privacy he enjoyed during his walks: "They do not consider that the wood-path and the boat are my studio, where I maintain a sacred solitude and cannot admit promiscuous company ... ask me for a certain number of dollars if you will, but do not ask me for my afternoons."

Although many adventures continued to occupy his life, when Thoreau turned thirty-four he began to regard his youth as a thing of the past, writing in his journal around the time of his birthday, "I think that no experience which I have today comes up to, or is comparable with, the experiences of my youth ... I can remember that I was all alive, and inhabited my body with inexpressible satisfaction." Thoreau may have been feeling older because he was not feeling well. He had all his teeth pulled that year and was fitted with a set of false teeth.

Despite his feelings of age, at this stage of his life, his journal reflects a preoccupation with all the beauties and sensations his five senses could perceive. He delighted in the purple stain left on his hand when he squeezed pokeberries; he noticed the scent of wild grapes in the air, and enjoyed the experience of swimming in the nude. When the first telegraph lines were strung through Concord in August 1851, Thoreau was further delighted to discover a new sound sensation. He had always loved the Aeolian harp—a tuning wire strung on a box and placed in a window to vibrate with the wind—and had built one for himself. Now he found that the telegraph wires made a gigantic Aeolian harp. "I put my ear to one of the posts," he said, "and it seemed to me as if every pore of the wood was filled with music, labored with the strain—as if every fibre was affected and being seasoned or timed, rearranged according to a new and more harmonious law."

In June of 1851, Thoreau was convinced that he needed to see his world by moonlight as well as sunlight to get a complete picture of it, and went for moonlight hikes all that summer. More and more, he wanted to know nature in every shape and form, and his journal became a catalog of his observations in the fields and woods and rivers of Concord.

Thoreau was increasingly preoccupied with the natural world. Nature provided him a glimpse of harmony and wonder that consistently stirred his mind and spirit. Although Thoreau never became so isolated that he rejected contact with other human beings, he found the human world far less harmonious and wonderful.

THOREAU AND OTHERS

By the late 1840s, Thoreau's friendship with Emerson had begun to cool; Emerson's career had reached its peak, but Thoreau was just beginning to come into his own intellectually, and he began to question Emerson's ideas with a new sense of self-confidence. Emerson, on the other hand, felt that Thoreau had not lived up to his hopes and expectations. Thoreau's only book had been a failure, and his name was hardly known outside of Concord. In his journal, Emerson complained: "Thoreau wants a little ambition in his mixture ... Instead of being the head of American engineers, he is captain of a huckleberry party."

In November of 1850, Thoreau expressed his own frustration when he wrote in his journal:

> I love my friends very much, but I find that it is of no use to go to see them. I hate them commonly when I am near them.

They belie themselves and deny me continually ... Even when I meet thee unexpectedly, I part from thee with disappointment. Though I enjoy thee more than other men, yet I am more disappointed with thee than with others.

Emerson, for his part, complained to others that Thoreau was never open, he did not know how to compromise, and he never bothered to please his friends. He apparently agreed with Elizabeth Hoar, who said, "I love Henry, but I can never like him."

Journal entries for Thoreau and Emerson from the same time period illustrate how differently they perceived their relationship. Emerson stated: "Henry does not feel himself except in opposition. He wants a fallacy to expose, a blunder to pillory, requires a little sense of victory, a roll of the drums, to call his powers into full exercise." Thoreau, on the other hand, wrote: "Talked, or tried to talk with R.W.E. Lost my time—nay, almost my identity. He, assuming a false opposition when there was no difference of opinion, talked to the wind—told me what I knew—and I lost my time trying to imagine myself somebody else to oppose him."

Journal entries from February of 1857 show that Thoreau felt his friendship with Emerson had come to an end. But apparently whatever words erupted between them released some pressure: "At the instant that I seem to be saying farewell forever to one who has been my friend I find myself unexpectedly near to him, and it is our very nearness and dearness to each other that gives depth and significance to that forever ... While I think I have broken one link, I have been forging another."

Thoreau and Emerson were able to build a new understanding, but it was never as close as the friendship they had once enjoyed. As time went on, Ellery Channing was more often the person with whom Thoreau took his walks and excursions. Channing was a moody, unpredictable sort of fellow who could be agreeable and generous one minute, and extremely selfish the next. The only person with whom he didn't quarrel was Thoreau.

By 1853, Channing's marriage was seriously troubled, and as he made no attempt to earn an income, his wife's family removed her and the children to live with them in Worcester. Channing made one unsuccessful attempt to gain custody of his children but was proven an unfit father. After this, Channing extended an invitation for Thoreau to live with him, but Thoreau refused, knowing Channing's troubles were more easily tolerated from a distance. Although he was genuinely fond of his friend, he was disgusted with Channing's treatment of his family.

Thoreau's care for his friends extended to human beings around the world. During the 1840s the potato famine in Ireland caused a great influx of Irish immigrants into New England, and Thoreau was among the very few who felt compassion for and championed this group of people. While most of his contemporaries were scornful of the Irish refugees, thinking them dirty and shiftless, Thoreau provided clothing or shoes when he saw a child without any; he loaned money to a family in need; and he even went door to door in an attempt to raise money for one family that was attempting to bring a family member from Ireland.

Thoreau was even more concerned about the plight of black people. In 1851 the Fugitive Slaw Law was passed, giving slave owners the right to seize and return runaway slaves with help from the federal government. This stirred the abolitionists' wrath, generating among them a greater commitment to intervening on the slaves' behalf. Thoreau and his family sheltered those seeking freedom and collected funds for them; Thoreau often accompanied black people who had escaped slavery to the train station, or even rode on the train with them for a while until they felt safe.

One particular incident infuriated Thoreau. Anthony Burns, a fugitive slave who worked at a clothing store in Boston, was confiscated by his former master and arrested. Abolitionists attempted to rescue him from jail, but President Franklin Pierce sent out the militia, and Burns was returned to slavery in Virginia. He was soon purchased by philanthropists and freed, but these events were fodder for Thoreau's speech "Slavery in Massachusetts." Thoreau affirmed in his speech, "The law will never make men free; it is men who have got to make the law free. They are the lovers of law and order who observe the law when the government breaks it." His speech attracted much attention and was published in the *Anti-Slavery Standard*, the *Liberator*, and the *Tribune*.

No matter how strongly Thoreau felt about an issue, he never joined any club or society designed to promote the ideals he felt so strongly. He was too much of an individualist; he needed to follow his own solitary route through life.

Children and young people delighted him; he liked their lack of pretension and their open minds. Although he had left the formal classroom behind, he continued to be an understanding and gentle teacher to the many children who sought him out.

Once, on a huckleberry picking expedition, when one of Emerson's young sons burst into inconsolable tears after tripping and spilling all his berries, Thoreau put his arm around the boy and explained that huckleberries would cease to grow if some were not planted each year; nature had provided for little boys who stumbled and sowed the berries. When the little boy came back in a few years, Thoreau promised, he would find berry bushes growing on the very spot where he had tripped.

Thoreau had by now written his first draft of *Walden* and had polished subsequent versions, adding passages and making changes after trying them out on the lecture platform. He submitted it to Ticknor & Fields of Boston, who had actually shown some interest in it in 1849. At that time, Thoreau had insisted that *A Week on the Concord and Merrimack Rivers* be published first. Now, the publisher was so taken with *Walden* that they offered Thoreau a 15 percent royalty rather than the standard 10 percent. Thoreau's old friend Horace Greeley publicized the book all spring prior to its publication, and it was officially published on August 9, 1854, in an edition of two thousand copies. Of the thirty-nine other books released that same year by Ticknor & Fields, *Walden* was the most famous.

Walden is Thoreau's account of the two years, two months, and two days he spent at Walden Pond. For artistic purposes, he condensed the narrative into the span of a single year. In the book, he did not advocate that civilization be abandoned and everyone flee to the woods. Instead, he advised:

> I would not have any one adopt *my* mode of living on any account; for beside that before he has fairly learned it I may have found out another for myself, I desire that there may be as many different persons in the world as possible; but I would have each one be very careful to find out and pursue *his own* way, and not his father's or his mother's or his neighbor's instead.

Although *Walden* can be read on many levels, at its deepest it is Thoreau's spiritual creed, his statement of faith. If human beings would obey the light of God within them, *Walden* affirmed, they could attain fulfillment and happiness. Thoreau was an optimist who believed humanity would someday follow the same light he had pursued so faithfully throughout his life.

Through *Walden*, Thoreau at last found the vehicle that allowed him to communicate his ideas to the world. The book did well, selling all but 256 copies of the original printing of two thousand in its first year, but by 1859 it was out of print and no longer available. Since 1861, however, it has never been out of print; it has been reprinted in more than 150 different editions and translated into virtually every major language.

Despite his new publishing success, Thoreau's life continued much as it always had. In 1852, through Bronson Alcott's intervention, Thoreau had the opportunity to survey land in New Jersey for a development designed for commuters from New York City. While he was in New York with Bronson Alcott, the two spent some time with Horace Greeley on his farm outside the city, and they also visited Walt Whitman, whose *Leaves of Grass* Thoreau had read.

Thoreau discovered that Whitman's habits and schedule of reading, writing, and walking were very similar to his own. While he and Whitman hesitated for some time on what to say and how to approach one another, they eventually conversed quite frankly, and Thoreau acknowledged to Whitman both his criticism and his admiration. Upon taking leave of each other, they exchanged books; Whitman gave Thoreau a copy of *Leaves of Grass* while Thoreau gave Whitman a copy of *A Week on the Concord and Merrimack Rivers*. Although they were not able to agree on certain points, they both had come to respect and admire each other.

In July of 1857, Thoreau and his cousin George Thatcher took their last trip to the Maine Woods, this time with a Native American guide named Joseph Polis. Polis had an extensive knowledge of the Indian language and more connection with the culture than any previous Indians Thoreau had come in contact with—the whole experience impressed him deeply. Polis took every opportunity to teach Thoreau his language, and also taught him how to paddle a canoe more efficiently by sliding the paddle back and forth along the canoe's side. Thoreau later wrote to Blake:

[The Indian] begins where we leave off. It is worth the while
to detect new faculties in man—he is so much the more

divine; and anything that fairly excites our admiration expands us. The Indian, who can find his way so wonderfully in the woods, possesses so much intelligence which the white man does not—and it increases my own capacity, as well as faith, to observe it. I rejoice to find that intelligence flows in other channels than I knew. It redeems for me portions of what seemed brutish before.

In September of 1857, James Russell Lowell, the editor of the newly established *Atlantic Monthly*, requested a contribution from Thoreau, who decided to submit the account of his 1853 excursion to Maine. It was to appear in installments, the first to be released in June. When the July installment came out, though, Thoreau discovered that Lowell had removed a sentence without consulting him. Thoreau wrote an angry letter to Lowell, but he made no correction to the manuscript, and neglected to answer Thoreau's letter.

Thoreau had made an enemy; Lowell's anger endured even after Thoreau's death. He denounced Thoreau as being a mere imitator of Emerson and dismissed his works as "one more symptom of the general liver complaint." Unfortunately for Thoreau, Lowell was an influential literary critic, and his opinions meant that Thoreau and his writing were not widely appreciated until decades later.

Thoreau's dealings with the outside world were often filled with conflict, but despite his frustrations and occasional misunderstandings, he continued to believe that human beings were capable of great things. This confidence endured in him even as he approached the last years of his life.

THOREAU'S LAST YEARS

On February 3, 1859, Thoreau's father passed away and Henry became the head of the family. The responsibility for the family business now fell on his shoulders.

Despite this new duty, Thoreau continued to be keenly involved in current events. When he heard about John Brown's raid on Harper's Ferry, Thoreau could think of nothing else; as much as he disliked the use of force and violence, he saw Brown as a man who was willing to sacrifice everything, even his life, for his principles. Shocked that no one defended Brown's actions, not even the abolitionists, he decided he had to speak up on Brown's behalf, and he prepared a lecture, which he delivered at the Concord Town Hall on October 30, 1859. His friends advised him not to speak, for fear he would further damage the antislavery movement, but he proceeded with his speech as planned. "A Plea for Captain John Brown" was one of his most passionate lectures.

Thoreau also continued his research of the American Indian. He collected Native American artifacts, and when Indians visited Concord in November 1850, he interviewed them on their hunting techniques, their clothing, and their woodcraft. By 1860 he had filled eleven notebooks with information on the American Indian, and although he was never able to turn his material into a book, he was one of the first white Americans to realize the worth of Native American cultures.

During this period of his life, he continued to lecture. Two of Thoreau's final lectures that were particularly popular were based on his essays "Wild Apples" and "The Succession of Forest Trees." "Wild Apples" was a work he had honed for many years, reworking and improving it until the end of his life. It was published in the *Atlantic Monthly* in November 1862, after his death.

His essay on "The Succession of Forest Trees" was given on September 20, 1860, in the Concord Town Hall before the Middlesex Agricultural Society. Thoreau had observed years earlier that trees would spring up in unlikely places, where there was no visible source of seed. Through continued observation, he concluded that animals such as squirrels were capable of carrying seeds very long distances, that wind could blow seeds hundreds of miles under the right conditions, and that even seeds blown off in the dust of railroad cars assisted in the dispersal. His surveying jobs gave him a great wealth of information, and he noted that if pines were cut down in a lot, oaks often came up in their place. "The Succession of Forest Trees" was Thoreau's contribution to scientific knowledge, and his conclusions are still accepted. The essay was published by Greeley in *The Weekly Tribune*.

Thoreau's fascination with the study of trees contributed to his final illness. Thoreau's family was apparently very susceptible to tuberculosis; it had been the cause of Henry's grandfather John Thoreau's death, and it contributed to his brother John's and his sister Helen's deaths. At the time, no one realized that it was a contagious condition, which made the disease harder to control. Thoreau may have lived as long as he did because he spent so much of his time outdoors in the fresh air, but years spent immersed in graphite dust undoubtedly had done nothing to help his condition. In December 1860, a cold he'd developed while studying tree rings eventually developed into bronchitis, further complicating his lifelong struggle with tuberculosis.

Ignoring the advice of his doctor, he insisted on keeping an appointment to deliver a lecture in Waterbury, Connecticut, on December 11, and by the time he returned home, he was gravely ill. He spent most of the winter inside, for the first time leaving large gaps between his journal entries. By the following April he was well enough to leave the house for brief strolls, but he found himself extremely sensitive to the cold. His doctor urged him to consider a dryer climate, such as the West Indies or Southern Europe, but Thoreau countered that those choices would be either too muggy or too expensive. He finally settled upon Minnesota as a likely spot, thinking the dry air there might improve his health.

Since he was not well enough to make the trip alone, he invited his friend Ellery Channing to come along, and when Channing could not make up his mind to go, he asked Blake. Blake could not make himself available on such short notice, and Thoreau invited Horace Mann Jr. (son of the educator), who had recently moved to Concord and had become acquainted with Thoreau because of their common interest in natural history.

The two left Concord on May 11, traveling through New York and stopping over at Niagara Falls for a night before continuing on to Chicago the next day. They crossed the Illinois prairie by train and finally arrived in St. Paul on May 26.

They spent nine days observing nature at Nicollet Island, Lake Calhoun, Minnehaha Falls, Hennepin Island, and along the banks of the Minnesota River, also enjoying an excursion up the Minnesota River on a steamboat to the Lower Sioux Agency near Redwood, where they watched the formal ceremonies that took place between Native Americans and white officials as the Indians received their payment from the federal government. In the afternoon a ceremonial dance was performed, followed by an ox roast.

On the trip home, Thoreau and Mann passed through Wisconsin, Milwaukee, Michigan, Toronto, and New York, and finally returned to Concord on July 9. The journey had not improved Thoreau's health; if anything, he had been worn down by the trip.

Thoreau's health continued to fail, but he made one last trip to New Bedford on August 19 to visit a friend. By the time he returned home he was much weakened, and he could no longer walk very far. His health seemed to improve a bit in October, but with the onset of cold weather again in November, his condition worsened. His last journal entry was made on November 3.

When his friends visited him, he told them, "Perhaps I am going up country." They noticed that "he seemed to be in an exalted state of mind for a long time before his death. He said it was just as good to be sick as to be well—just as good to have a poor time as a good time."

That last winter, despite his illness, Thoreau continued his literary efforts. The *Atlantic Monthly*, which had been taken over by Ticknor & Fields, the publishers of *Walden*, solicited him for contributions, and since James Russell Lowell was no longer there as editor, Thoreau agreed to submit several of his essays, all of which were published before his death. Ticknor & Fields also made arrangements to have both *Walden* and *A Week on the Concord and Merrimack Rivers* reprinted.

He grew gradually weaker, though, and he could not continue to write for long. His sister Sophia said of Thoreau's last days:

> Now the embodiment of weakness; still, he enjoys seeing his friends, and every bright hour he devotes to his manuscripts which he is preparing for publication. For many weeks he has spoken only in a faint whisper. Henry accepts this dispensation with such childlike trust and is so happy that I feel as if he were being translated rather than dying in the ordinary way of most mortals.

Although they knew he was dying, Thoreau's friends and neighbors did not shy away but visited him frequently. One visitor commented that he "never saw a man dying with so much pleasure and peace."

When another visitor said to him, "Well, Mr. Thoreau, we must all go," Thoreau replied, "When I was a very little boy I learned that I must die, and I set that down, so of course I am not disappointed now. Death is as near to you as it is to me."

Some of Thoreau's visitors were concerned about the state of his soul, but he had no such concerns. His personal religion remained unorthodox to the end. When an old woman, a friend of the family, asked him if he was right with Jesus, he told her that he found more spiritual meaning in a snowstorm than he did in Christ—and when his Aunt Louisa asked him if he had made his peace with God, he answered, "I did not know we had ever quarreled, Aunt."

Thoreau died on May 6, 1862, when he was forty-four years old. Emerson delivered his eulogy, ending with this thought: "His soul was made for the noblest society; he had in a short life exhausted the capabilities of this world; wherever there is knowledge, wherever there is virtue, wherever there is beauty, he will find a home."

Henry David Thoreau: Bachelor of Thought and Nature

INTRODUCTION

Thoreau's accomplishments as a writer and a naturalist, and his surprisingly far-reaching political influence, are rarely disputed. His lasting importance could be established on the basis of "Civil Disobedience" alone; Ghandi and Martin Luther King Jr. both traced their nonviolent tactics and the basic elements of their political philosophies largely from this single essay. However, there has endured from his own time to the present a considerable variety of opinion regarding Thoreau's philosophical worth, his consistency of argument, and even his personality. Does he present a clear philosophy in his writings? Do the facts of his life express or belie his ideas? Was he a prickly misanthrope, a pessimist, a narcissist?

In *Walden*'s first paragraph, he writes: "In most books, the I, or first person, is omitted; in this it will be retained ..." By making himself the subject of *Walden*, his masterpiece, Thoreau invites the reader to speculate about the author, and to compare his explicit self-representation with the somewhat broader, more commodious portrait we may derive from observing his performance. Much of the evidence employed by those critics looking to deflate *Walden* is supplied by Thoreau himself; if he intended to misrepresent or idealize himself in certain ways, he did a poor job of hiding his irregularities.

Thoreau's lesser-known first book, *A Week on the Concord and Merrimack Rivers*, is a journeyman work, loosely constructed and somewhat unevenly realized. It opens with several original verses which include the line "Be thou my Muse, my Brother." Although seldom mentioned in the narrative, Thoreau's brother John was his companion on the river trip he recounts. Shortly after their return, John died suddenly in the first days of 1842. Thoreau was so deeply affected by his brother's illness that he exhibited the symptoms himself, and his brother's death plunged him into a protracted period of mourning. *A Week on the Concord and Merrimack Rivers* is something of a memorial to his brother, albeit a subtle one. Thoreau does not describe his brother, choosing instead to narrate around him, perhaps with the intention of recovering something of his brother's presence indirectly, unmediated by any attempt on his part to define it.

John Thoreau also haunts his brother's poetry, although he was not its sole subject. Critical opinion of Thoreau's poetry in general has been mixed; but, while his use of rhyme and meter is conventional and even sing-song in some instances, his verse is nevertheless marked by the striking natural imagery (the fog he calls "Thou wind-blown meadow of the air"), the blunt, frank tone, and the economically direct address that distinguish his prose. Both in verse and in prose, Thoreau's writing is disciplined and sure-minded, studded with surprising imagery, dry wit (often unnoticed by critics, who proclaim with James Russell Lowell, "Thoreau has no humor"), and a kind of argument from common sense that Mark Twain would put to good use a generation later. This poem, entitled "Independence," is a fair specimen of Thoreau's poetry, and of his numerous manifestos as well:

> My life more civil is and free
> Than any civil polity.
>
> Ye princes keep your realms
> And circumscribed power,
> Nor wide as are my dreams,
> Nor rich as is this hour.
>
> What can ye give which I have not?
> What can ye take which I have got?

Can ye defend the dangerless?
Can ye inherit nakedness?

To all true wants time's ear is deaf,
Penurious states lend no relief
Out of their pelf—
But a free soul—thank God—
Can help itself.

Be sure your fate
Doth keep apart its state—
Not linked with any band—
Even the nobles of the land.

In tented fields with cloth of gold—
No place doth hold
But is more chivalrous than they are.
And sigheth for a nobler war.
A finer strain its trumpet rings—
A brighter gleam its armor flings.

The life that I aspire to live
No man proposeth me—
No trade upon the street
Wears its emblazonry.

While Thoreau wrote three other volumes (two of which were published posthumously—*The Maine Woods* and *Cape Cod*), published many of his poems, maintained a detailed journal for most of his life, and delivered numerous lectures on diverse topics, *Walden* assumes paramount importance in any consideration of Thoreau's literary career. As his most sustained treatment of the philosophical concerns that meant the most to him, it is the lens through which all his other writings are read. The following sections will deal with three of Thoreau's principal themes.

RESTORATION

America was not immediately affected by the new German philosophy of the latter decades of the eighteenth century, nor was the effect uniform from region to region when it began to be felt. The systems and ideas put forward by Immanuel Kant, Goethe, Friedrich and August Schlegel, and others, eventually reached America in the 1820s and 1830s, and were recommended to educated American readers by virtue of the influence they had already exerted on the English Romantics.

Samuel Taylor Coleridge was the principal interpreter of German philosophy to much of the English-speaking world, and after him, the fiery and popular (if controversial) Thomas Carlyle. One of Carlyle's longest-suffering friends and correspondents was an American who, when they met, was already beginning to enjoy fame at home and even abroad as a public speaker and moralist: Ralph Waldo Emerson. He, in turn, would become the center of New England's own particular version of Romanticism; a movement known as Transcendentalism.

While its enthusiastic correspondents were drawn from the bookish set of Boston and especially Cambridge, Transcendentalism's recognized home was the bucolic town of Concord, where Emerson lived. Thoreau was not only born in Concord but almost never removed himself from it; his attachment to Emerson personally was hardly less stubborn. From their first acquaintance, Thoreau was a constant presence in Emerson's life, and vice versa. In effect, he appeared to carry on a private, internal colloquy with Emerson for the rest of his life; perhaps Thoreau could never entirely get over the fact that Emerson had articulated and anticipated his own unexamined, spontaneous philosophy.

His career as a writer can be understood as an ongoing campaign to reclaim his own ideas, wresting them out of Emerson's expressions. Thoreau did not, however, seem to be particularly troubled by the tendency of many of his contemporaries to see him as Emerson's personal echo. While their points in common may be more obvious to later readers, Emerson was, at the time, characterized by hostile onlookers as a dreamy, vague thinker who never descended from the clouds to contend with the business of life.

Thoreau's approach was, on the contrary, occupied with concrete things. Nevertheless, redundancy with Emerson was one of the more facile means employed by editors and journalists looking for an excuse to dismiss Thoreau unexamined. In fact, despite the obvious importance of Emerson's example in Thoreau's life, the two of them owed their points in common to the shared philosophical legacy of Transcendentalism itself. They were among the first to join American voices to an ongoing and vigorous philosophical conversation that had commenced in Germany in the late eighteenth century, and had been taken up by the English Romantics in the subsequent generation.

Goethe generated an interest in nature and speculative knowledge, the confidence that spirit and science are not necessarily at odds, and a cosmic sweep in artistic rendering. For the cult that grew up around Goethe after his death, he was the last great Renaissance man; his genius had borne fruit in the arts, in the sciences, and in philosophy. Such versatility was an indication of universality, a mind that could be commensurate with all of existence. Goethe himself was several shades more modest than this, but he did give to the Transcendentalists a model of the self-made and self-reliant intellect. Much of the Romantic preoccupation with the self, with self-knowledge and self-cultivation (even becoming one's own work of art), is due to Goethe's influence. This self-involvement is plain in Thoreau's work, as is Goethe's versatility; Thoreau wrote prose and verse, and made his own contributions to science and politics.

Kant provided Emerson with the term "transcendental," referring to a kind of knowledge that is certain although intuitive (Kant himself did not believe this kind of knowledge to be truly possible). From Kant also came insistence upon the absolute freedom of the individual. For him, freedom and morality were reciprocally dependent, and he understood morality to be reason in practice. Furthermore, the complete independence and distinctness of the individual was such that no one could presume to speak for another, to characterize the experience of another.

While Kant himself would not have gone so far, most of his German interpreters and their English audience drew the conclusion from him that truth was always personal, never abstract, because it must always be found in the experience of an individual. Where science spoke of "facts," the Romantics and Transcendentalists spoke of *truths*: facts which have not been divorced from the subjective experience that led to their discovery. This would be one of the central theses of Thoreau's philosophy: that freedom, self-reliance, and the cultivation of one's own truth are all bound up together.

Finally, from the Schlegel brothers came a new, partial, and fragmentary approach to philosophy. The a priori (proceeding from first concepts, as opposed to proceeding from experience) philosophical system, complete and oppressively exhaustive, had been the chief aim of Enlightenment philosophy. The Schlegels argued that, the infinite universe being far too vast and complex to be apprehended by any limited mind, the best understanding of the cosmos, of God, would take these limits into account in its representation. Any representation of the infinite must be itself infinite, not finite and not finished, but fragmentary. The fragment stands open on the edge of the infinite, and is a symbol of it.

Thoreau often saw in his natural surroundings a set of signs that seemed to be symbols of God; in the spontaneous order and balance of nature, he saw in microcosm a sign of a greater universal order and balance. While Thoreau's sense of the cosmic seems impaired by a tendency to measure everything according to his own scale, the sense of Schlegel's infinite mystery does appear, for example, in his description of the forbidding Mount Katahdin in *The Maine Woods*. The mountain is excessive, dangerous, unyielding, representing nature's disturbing indifference and overwhelming power. For Thoreau, Katahdin is the exception, and the balanced, accommodating nature of Walden Pond and its woody surroundings is the rule.

Thoreau certainly did not set out to establish a complete system of universally-binding truth, either from first principles or experience, but rather insisted on a freedom that must be the necessary precondition of any truth. If the whole could be apprehended at once, then it would appear in contemplation, in passive observation—not in active accumulation of facts, fitting data into a pre-established pattern.

Emerson read Eastern philosophy in tandem with Western, and Thoreau availed himself of Emerson's small collection of translated Indian and Chinese classics and frequently quoted them (Confucius in particular) in his writings. The attitude of contemplative passivity and receptiveness pervading these books was, for Thoreau, a tonic answer to the acquisitive, active, aggressive mood of American popular rhetoric at the time. In his essay "Life Without Principle" he wrote, "I think that there is nothing, not even crime, more opposed to poetry, to philosophy, ay, to life itself, than this incessant business." Time and again, Thoreau would return to this fundamental theme: that Americans foolishly waste their lives in pursuit of worthless and unnecessary things, simply because they never permit themselves to pause and reflect on their values. The lesson to be learned in nature is that life will sustain itself, and easily. "Probably I should not consciously and deliberately forsake my particular calling to do the good which society demands of me, to save the universe from annihilation; and I believe that a like but infinitely greater steadfastness elsewhere is all that now preserves it." (*Walden*, 380)

Like all real philosophies, Transcendentalism was not merely a new way of organizing, understanding, and perceiving, but a new way of life. It aimed at the restoration of a universal unity into which man alone had introduced arbitrary and short-sighted distinctions; nature, man, and God are all of a piece.

In his influential *Leviathan*, English philosopher Thomas Hobbes characterized human life as "nasty, brutish, and short." This point of view, which regarded the natural state of affairs as a savage chaos, dominated much of English and American thought about nature for nearly a century; having read Jean-Jacques Rousseau, the Romantics in Europe and the Transcendentalists in America held the inverse view. Society, they said, corrupts and demoralizes mankind. Nature is innocent and orderly by comparison. So the Transcendentalists tended to take the side of nature against town and city, against society, and none more so than Thoreau. Turning away from society requires great inner resourcefulness. With the Kant-derived notion that all truth is personal and subjective, Thoreau, like many others of this time, retired from society in order to find his own truth, and to achieve as much self-reliance as possible.

What, according to Thoreau, were the stakes in the struggle with society's enforced conformity of opinion, of unexamined truth? He described what he felt he stood to regain in this allegorical passage from *Walden*:

> I long ago lost a hound, a bay horse, and a turtledove, and am still on their trail. Many are the travelers I have spoken to concerning them, describing their tracks and what calls they answered to. I have met one or two who had heard the

hound, and the tramp of the horse, and even seen the dove disappear behind a cloud, and they seemed as anxious to recover them as if they had lost them themselves. (*Walden*, 336)

The hound is love and good fellowship; the horse, health and strength; and the dove, faith and compassion. It's no coincidence that Thoreau uses animals to represent what has been lost to civilized, invalided, selfish mankind.

In the course of eighteen chapters, *Walden* gives an account of a year spent by the pond. The year is an organic unit of time; Thoreau's doesn't begin in January but in early summer. He will measure time according to the seasons, not by the standard, artificial scale of the calendar. Following the course of *Walden's* year, we pass from the accomplished ripeness of summer, through the dying season of autumn, into the dead of winter, to emerge finally in the rebirth of spring. "As every season seems best to us in its turn, so the coming in of spring is like the creation of Cosmos out of Chaos and the realization of the Golden Age." (*Walden*, 572) The correlation of the content of *Walden* to the changing seasons reflects Thoreau's transcendental purpose: to proclaim that the restoration of something like Eden is possible for mankind.

From the point of view of conventional religion, there appears to be something blasphemous in this statement. Most Christian denominations accept as doctrine the restoration of Eden after the last judgment, but this restoration is brought about by God, not, or at least not entirely, by man. On closer examination, the restoration that is *Walden's* most important theme is, for Thoreau, the realization of God's will as expressed in nature. Eden is already available. Nature is God's Providence to mankind, and observing it in its orderly operation, its economy and simplicity, is education enough in how God intends man to live. Therefore Thoreau is not vulnerable to the criticism that his espoused restoration is man striving to reverse or defy the will of God, as some claimed.

He did, however, deny the concept of original sin and its expression in man as an innate depravity, the cornerstone of the Calvinist theology upon which the New England colonies were originally founded. Man's evil is man-made, and therefore can be unmade by man.

Whatever else may befall mankind will come from nature, and nature, being innately balanced, cannot be unjust.

We must also distinguish *Walden*'s restoration from the schemes of the many utopian or reformist movements of the middle and late nineteenth century. From their point of view, the ineluctable advance of progress, the development of the sciences, of industry, of political and other institutions, would (to present the case simply) lead to the formation of a state in which at least some perennial social problems and inequalities would be permanently resolved. Thoreau's restoration, on the other hand, is a matter of simplification; specifically, it restores innocence, which, for Thoreau, is simplicity, naturalness.

Thoreau's thought on this subject resembles Rousseau's and reproduces in its own way the same dialectic development. An unselfconscious and therefore unvalued innocence gives way, in the assembly of any polity, to guilt, shame, social status, complex self-justifications and excuses; however, the original innocence is recognized only from the point of view of this fallen condition, and its value acknowledged. It clears the way for the restoration of innocence, but an innocence modified by the broader scheme in which it now takes its place: a selfconscious innocence, one that knows its own worth because it has experienced the alternative. In other words, we could say one must go into town in order to recognize the value of the country. Thenceforth, the most desirable way to proceed would bring the perspective gained by the trip into town back into the country. Innocence becomes a choice, and a discipline.

Thoreau revises the familiar trope of man's fall. It would be inconsistent with his individualistic philosophy to suppose that the fault of an ancestor, even the first, could be binding on succeeding generations. The fall of mankind is not a single event in the past, but an aggregate of individual lapses in the present. Each individual falls out of nature and into society's delirium. Some emerge from illusion only to fall back a second time; some are forever relapsing. No state or institution can permanently resolve this problem; rather, an unwavering mindfulness on the part of the individual is required (this is plainly a more active Western application of an Eastern idea). It may be impossible to avoid forgetting and lapsing again into delusion, but if one is constantly reminding oneself of the truth, this forgetting can be countered.

Parallel to this cycle of falling and recovering, Thoreau follows a second dialectical movement through the passage of autumn and winter to spring, through death to a new birth. Thoreau does not identify natural death and decay with the social corruption of humanity, however. Thoreau's approach to death bolsters his restoration argument; death, which seems to negate life, is instead plainly necessary to life and bound up with life. If death is a part of life, then it becomes possible to see life and death as a whole. Death ceases to be the antagonist of life, becoming instead its bridge to an infinite scheme of death and rebirth.

Likewise, the unnatural state of unexamined society is not the antagonist of the natural, innocent state of man, because the route to a new and higher innocence passes directly through society. If the fallout of natural spontaneity into social automatism (a kind of spiritual death) is an irrevocable step, then it would be impossible to achieve a new innocence by means of this fall. By making it instead the necessary precondition for this new innocence, as death is to new life, Thoreau avoids making this paradox. Social automatism is not a crime, it is an error, a falling asleep. Spring is the sign that death is not final; likewise, the spiritual death represented by the fall is not final.

What Thoreau proposes is not an immediate moral amelioration, like that proposed by so many evangelical and utopian reformers, but rather an alteration in perspective which will in turn result in better morals. When one no longer blindly gropes after wealth and status and luxuries, or pretends to enjoy what only brings pain to oneself and others, one will no longer have any cause to covet a neighbor's property, to rob, coerce, or enslave.

UNITY OF EXPERIENCE AND THOREAU'S POLITICS

Emerson called Thoreau "the bachelor of Thought and Nature"—"a born protestant" who "interrogated every custom ... as if he did not feel himself except in opposition." Many critics regard Thoreau's dogged individualism as a matter of temperament, or even of bravado. The obvious self-confidence that epitomizes his literary tone is as much an element of his philosophy as it is an aspect of his character, however.

Thoreau launched himself into experience without endeavoring to second-guess it, to organize or systematize it in any extensive way, with supreme confidence in the transcendent unity of nature and of the individual. One need only recount one's experience honestly, thoroughly, and without prejudgment, and its own organic, inherent structure, its unity, will emerge on its own. For Thoreau, both writing and sojourning, either in the woods or in town, were experiments whose results were in doubt from the outset, but allowed to mature of their own accord.

Thoreau and Emerson both are frequently taken to task for inconsistencies and contradictions that appear in any broad survey of their writings. Emerson said that "a foolish consistency is the hobgoblin of small minds." In his "Song of Myself," Walt Whitman, who was not strictly numbered among the Transcendentalists but was acquainted with many of them and echoed them in his own thinking, put it like this: "I contradict myself? / Very well then I contradict myself, / (I am large, I contain multitudes.)" While the sentiment is not precisely the same, the air of confident indifference to inconsistency is.

In his eulogy, Emerson also noted that, for Thoreau, the fact is "a type of order and beauty of the whole." There can be no need to systematize in advance, for the "system" will take care of itself. This aspect of Transcendentalism, later known as "personalism," holds that truth does not exist independently of persons, and conversely, the truth is therefore always personal. It isn't attached to a person, as if external, but is a part of him—it is the soul or essence of that person. So, any expression of truth is an expression of soul (and of self, leading many readers somewhat hastily to call Thoreau a narcissist).

This also means that the truth may not always exactly coincide with the facts; *Walden* itself, for example, was not written during Thoreau's stay in the hut by Walden Pond, but afterwards, at his mother's house. In his naturalistic essay "Dispersion of Seeds," he puts the point simply: "I do not always state the facts exactly in the order in which they were observed but select out of my numerous observations extended over a series of years the most important ones and describe them in a natural order."

The flowering of the fact into a truth (a metaphor which Thoreau employed in his first published essay "The Natural History of Massachusetts") is a matter of making information into experience. As a young man, Thoreau was dismissed from his post as a schoolteacher for refusing to employ physical punishment as part of his discipline. For a brief period thereafter, he and his brother set up and ran their own school; there was no physical punishment, and students were given longer recesses and field trips.

In *Walden*, Thoreau makes a passing reference to his philosophy of schooling; students "should not *play* life, or *study* it merely, while the community supports them at this expensive game, but earnestly *live* it from beginning to end." (*Walden*, 363) At a time when schoolchildren spent the bulk of their time in rote memorization and repetitive exercises, Thoreau emphasized the importance of experience, the cultivation of a faculty for firsthand observation and the insistence upon seeing for oneself. Above all, the student must understand how what he learns will affect him in his everyday practices.

The practical application of transcendental theories of knowledge and experience drew the Transcendentalists themselves to political reform. Thoreau observed, "I know of no more encouraging fact than the unquestionable ability of man to elevate his life by conscious endeavor ..." (*Walden*, 395) He had no use for professional reformers or clergy, or for politicians. "If I knew for a certainty that a man was coming to my house with the conscious design of doing me good, I should run for my life ..." (*Walden*, 381) Parties, doctrines, and organizations he regarded as useful but dangerous tools, even as weapons of last resort.

Between his birth in 1817 and the publication of *Walden* in 1854, Thoreau saw the population of the United States more than double, growing from under ten million to over twenty-three million. He witnessed the annexation of Texas, Arizona, New Mexico, California, and Oregon. He saw the advent of the locomotive and the telegraph, and he was concerned by the reorientation of American culture toward the accumulation of wealth. In "Life Without Principle" he wrote: "The ways by which you may get money almost without exception lead downward. To have done anything by which you earned money *merely* is to have been truly idle or worse."

If experience is properly a unified whole, then no one element of life can be entirely divorced from any other. Thoreau's spiritual strivings therefore expressed themselves in his diet, his budget, his hours of waking and sleeping, his work and his rest. *Walden*'s first chapter is entitled "Economy," and Thoreau is perhaps best known for his spartan disregard for material wealth. The quest for self owes a great deal to Romanticism, but it is not marked by the same sense of desire, and will, that characterizes the Romantic quest. Rather, Thoreau was always detaching his desire, his will, from those objects of social value he called "luxuries" and adhering them instead to simple, natural things. "Most of the luxuries, and many of the so called comforts of life, are not only not indispensable, but positive hinderances to the elevation of mankind. With respect to luxuries and comforts, the wisest have ever lived a more simple and meagre life than the poor." (*Walden*, 334) This was perhaps the most fundamental way in which he translated the somewhat abstract Romantic and Transcendental notions of the search for the self into concrete practices.

Freedom—the state of being free—is always attainable; anyone at any time can refuse to go along with the crowd. Society is forever erasing consciousness of an innate freedom—or, more subtly, promoting the idea that freedom is a luxury to be earned; therefore, perhaps freedom is purchased with wealth. One is unfree now, so as to be free later—but as a rule, "later" never comes. As a result, "the mass of men lead lives of quiet desperation." (*Walden*, 329) Thoreau would say, rather, that all persons have the freedom to earn or not to earn, to join society or to remain aloof, and that this freedom is perennial.

Thoreau does not propose to abandon society as such, but to live in it without being of it; in other words, without forgetting one is always free to choose, to withdraw. The great threat of society is its power to make individuals act without reflection, its subtle intimidations and invisible coercions. The refrain "mass of men" returns in this quote from "Civil Disobedience": "the mass of men serve the state thus, not as men mainly, but as machines, with their bodies."

By refusing to pay his poll tax and insisting that he be hauled off to jail, Thoreau compelled society—in this case, the town of Concord—to resort to obvious force to keep him in line. Martin Luther King Jr. and Mohandas K. Gandhi both employed the same means in their liberation struggles: their blatant but nonviolent disobedience left authority no choice but to use equally blatant repression to maintain itself. In the process, the truth is unambiguously revealed that society depends upon certain conformities, and will use violence when necessary to impose itself on its citizens, even those who act with the full approval of their own consciences.

For Thoreau, the most desperate political struggle of the time was plainly the controversy over slavery, and he was, if anything, more vehement in his criticism of complacent, do-nothing Northerners than he was of the Southern slaveholders themselves. He wrote in "Civil Disobedience":

> Practically speaking, the opponents to a reform in Massachusetts are not a hundred thousand politicians at the South, but a hundred thousand merchants and farmers here, who are more interested in commerce and agriculture than they are in humanity, and are not prepared to do justice to the slave and to Mexico [the United States, employing very flimsy pretexts, had declared war on Mexico at the time, for the purpose of territorial expansion], *cost what it may*. I quarrel not with far-off foes, but with those who, near at home, co-operate with, and do the bidding of, those far away, and without whom the latter would be harmless.

When John Brown attempted to foment a slave rebellion by seizing the United States armory in Harper's Ferry, Virginia, some abolitionists in the North joined the general chorus of dismayed voices condemning Brown from pulpits and editorial pages. While they had to recognize his commendable and unquestionably complete commitment to ending slavery, abolitionists were appalled by his violent means. But as the Northern reformers expressed their reservations, Thoreau grew only more insistent in broadcasting his unqualified admiration for Brown from the podium of the Concord Lyceum. "The man this country was about to hang appeared the greatest and best in it." ("John Brown")

While not a violent man himself, Thoreau apparently regarded violence as nothing too aberrant or unnatural. Brown's high-minded defiance, his unrelenting courage—both moral and physical—spoke directly to Thoreau's sensibilities. Above all, he was affected by Brown's decision to change the country by himself, as a single individual of conscience. John Brown's contribution to American history alone guaranteed that his name would be remembered by following generations. That he is popularly regarded by many as a martyr to the abolitionist cause is due to the work of a particular body of writers, with Thoreau in their vanguard.

As for philanthropists, Thoreau regarded them with skepticism, if not with cynicism. "If you give money, spend yourself with it, and do not merely abandon it [to the recipient] ... I want the flower and fruit of a man; that some fragrance be wafted over from him to me, and some ripeness flavor our intercourse. His goodness must not be a partial and transitory act, but a constant superfluity, which costs him nothing and of which he is unconscious. This is a charity that hides a multitude of sins." (*Walden*, 383) In other words, the philanthropist, the benefactor of mankind, operates almost entirely in the abstract, helping "the Poor" or "the People," but never confronting them as individuals. Thoreau would rather do without such help and the obligation it entails, preferring instead the "superfluity" or surplus of another, freely given and freely received, without obligation—an exchange between equals.

Although he did not himself coin the phrase, Thoreau is often associated with the words "That government governs best which governs least." They occur in the first paragraph of "Civil Disobedience," and Thoreau goes on to say that, in his opinion, "That government governs best which governs not at all."

This should not be mistaken for a call to abolish government altogether. While some choose to regard Thoreau as merely a negative voice, offering criticisms of the existing polity without positing any alternative, Thoreau in fact made his political position very clear. He wanted a noncoercive, cooperative government that permitted the individual free self-determination; he believed in a lasting, friendly antagonism between citizen and system in which the citizen received the benefit of the doubt.

He accepted the necessity of compulsory education, of government measures to preserve natural resources and defend the population by putting out fires, solving crimes, laying and maintaining roads, and issuing correct maps. However, he believed the government should not "govern" the actions of individuals; rather, the opposite should obtain: "There will never be a really free and enlightened State until the State comes to recognize the individual as a higher and independent power, from which all its own power and authority are derived, and treats him accordingly."

EXPERIMENT AND OBSERVATION

This passage is the core of the chapter entitled "Where I Lived, and What I Lived For," and succinctly expresses Thoreau's project in *Walden*:

I went to the woods because I wished to live deliberately, to
front only the essential facts of life, and see if I could not
learn what it had to teach, and not, when I came to die,
discover that I had not lived. I did not wish to live what was
not life, living is so dear; nor did I wish to practice
resignation, unless it was quite necessary. I wanted to live
deep and suck out all the marrow of life, to live so sturdily
and Spartan-like as to put to rout all that was not life, to cut
a broad swath and shave close, to drive life into a corner, and
reduce it to its lowest terms, and, if it proved to be mean, why
then to get the whole and genuine meanness of it, and
publish its meanness to the world; or if it were sublime, to
know it by experience, and be able to give a true account of
it in my next excursion. (*Walden*, 395)

So *Walden* is an expedition to find the basics of human life. To
know by experience is something more true, and of greater scope and
depth, than knowledge by abstract reasoning. Facts are articles of
abstract reasoning, but they are also components of truths. Truth does
not stand opposed to fact; rather, the fact is an embryonic truth.

Thoreau did not disdain facts as such, nor did he dismiss scientific
inquiry out of hand—in fact, Thoreau himself made significant
contributions to science. The word "experiment" recurs throughout
Thoreau's works; insofar as scientific practice abides by the rules of
methodological objectivity, observing without prejudging, it could lead
to the discovery of truths by means of facts.

However, as in his political philosophy, Thoreau believed in a
nonbinding arrangement with science itself. Just as the citizen must
examine every policy of the government in turn and determine whether
or not to cooperate based on a sense of the "higher law," never forgetting
that governments and laws are provisional, so the scientific observer
must never forget that scientific theories, laws, and especially
institutions, are likewise provisional. In science, as in politics, one owes
one's first loyalty to the truth, the higher law, and none at all to tradition,
rules, or theories. Even the most soundly-based theories are liable to
change, and can only be truths, properly speaking, in experience. In his
naturalistic essays, Thoreau doesn't seem to expect the reader to accept
his observations merely by virtue of his report. His essays are essentially

guides, indicating those things that anyone would notice in passing through the woods, and inviting readers to go and to see for themselves.

In part, Thoreau insists on the provisional nature of knowledge to prevent it from obscuring experience. (He certainly felt that science is not alone sufficient for understanding experience, but only certain aspects of it. The individual, in particular, is not subject matter for scientific analysis.) When one takes it for granted that something is known and familiar, one ceases to see it. "If men would steadily observe realities only, and not allow themselves to be deluded, life, to compare it with such things as we know, would be like a fairy tale and the Arabian Nights' Entertainments." (*Walden*, 398) The richness of experience has less to do with its content than with the intensity of the subject's awareness.

Many Transcendentalists used the contemplation of nature as a springboard to catch some glimpse of the infinite. Thoreau understood why, but with this qualification: "In eternity there is indeed something true and sublime. But all these times and places and occasions are now and here. God himself culminates in the present moment, and will never be more divine in the lapse of all the ages." (*Walden*, 399) The experience of the here and now is ordinary, not exotic.

If the term "mystic" is used to describe Thoreau (and he applied the word to himself), it must be received as having an almost technically precise meaning. The perception of the infinite by natural signs does not entail any extraordinary sense; perception is ordinary. One sees the tree, the water, the bird, in the usual way. Rather, it is that the usual, ordinary way of seeing takes on a deeper significance. So, rather than seeking an extraordinary vision that will transcend a vulgar, banal, sensory world, Thoreau is pointing out that ordinary vision, like a simple life, is entirely sufficient when unobstructed by delusions.

People live among phantoms, and do not really see the world at all; when they go in search of it, they typically find only a different set of phantoms and dream worlds. Those who have trained themselves to see what lies immediately around them have a far richer world in their view than anyone could dream. Seeking the world, in fact, is a strange idea: as if one's world were somewhere else, not here and now. Perception is itself whole, and not divided into specialized parts—this for seeing the divine, that for dealing with the everyday; this for man, that for nature— so Thoreau did not discriminate between his studies of the woods and his studies of his neighbors: "As I walked in the woods to see the birds and squirrels, so I walked in the village to see the men and boys ..." (*Walden*, 456)

Before *Walden*, Thoreau had already earned a local reputation as an amateur naturalist, at a time when the study of nature had not yet become exclusively the province of professionals. Emerson, in his eulogy, spoke of Thoreau's prodigious knowledge of and near-instinctive familiarity with the natural landscape in Concord. "It was a pleasure and a privilege to walk with him. He knew the country like a fox or a bird, and passed through it as freely by paths of his own. He knew every track in the snow or on the ground, and what creature had taken this path before him. One must submit abjectly to such a guide, and the reward was great."

After the publication of *Walden*, Thoreau's involvement with the proper study of natural history continued to deepen. In 1850 he wrote in his journal:

> I feel that the character of my knowledge is from year to year becoming more distinct and scientific; that, in exchange for views as wide as heaven's scope, I am being narrowed down to the field of the microscope. I see details, not wholes nor the shadow of the whole. I count some parts, and say, "I know."

His later journals are more like account books, replete with extended descriptions of plants and animals, of weather and terrain; and they, like his essays, make constant reference to scientific books and journals. Thoreau was trained as a surveyor, and *Walden* features a precisely measured and sounded map of the pond itself. He corresponded with Agassiz, the famous Swiss naturalist working in the United States, and in 1847 sent him numerous specimens of plants and animals, some of which were the first cataloged of their species.

In 1850 he was elected to the Boston Society of Natural History as a corresponding member, and began to pursue a systematic curriculum of naturalist readings. He was appointed to the Harvard College Committee for Examination in Natural History in 1859. His essay on forest tree succession is considered by many today as the standard treatment of the subject. But for all this close cooperation, when Agassiz and his associates set about professionalizing the discipline of natural history, Thoreau kept his distance, and did not participate in the institutionalization of the science. When the Association for the Advancement of Science offered him a membership, he declined, writing, "I am a mystic, a transcendentalist, and a natural philosopher to boot."

Thoreau was punctiliously wary of falling into what William Blake called "single vision": to take only one point of view on something is to accept as complete an incomplete picture. While he became steadily more involved with natural history, collecting specimens and observing animal behavior, he never adopted the scientific style of description. His reports, while they may be terse and factual, never pretend to pure objectivity, as if the question of their origin, the identity and personality of the observer, were irrelevant.

As was the case with art and with philosophy, so with science too there is a tendency to try to predetermine the experience. Thoreau believed it was better, truer, to remain passive. The experience has a higher accuracy than the accurately-expressed fact, because it does not attempt the quixotic task of removing the observer and his personhood from the scene, does not ask us to pretend that the observer is a transparent nobody. As in other aspects of his life, Thoreau did not so much enter into the scientific enterprise as observe it from without, mindful of the moral issues involved. Facts are partial, bits of information that must not be mistaken for the whole, for truth, which is found only in experience, and which requires no professional competence or university training to perceive.

During the 1860s the field of natural history was beginning to constrict, becoming less a matter of collection and identification and more a matter of a fixed university curriculum, a professional specialty. Thoreau had no interest in professions as such, and remained aloof. He belonged to the last generation that could pursue and make significant contributions to naturalistic science as amateurs, as lay contributors. Ultimately, Thoreau took the interpretation of science, its communication with poetry and a humanistic philosophy, more seriously than any specific contribution he might have made.

SUMMATION

Some critics indict Thoreau for being a false prophet, a performer caricaturing "the philosopher" or "the hermit," perhaps in a shortsighted, hero-worshipping imitation of Emerson. Thoreau made his life the principal exercise-ground of his philosophy. He did not decide in advance of experience what he believed the best life to be, but set out to discover it in the most reduced circumstances he could procure for himself. His life in the woods was, in part, an exercise in Stoicism, but it was no less an attempt to grasp what was most essential in life, the better to live in and around society. This is why he did not permanently remove himself to the shores of Walden Pond.

It should surprise no one that there would be mistakes, irregularities, and pretense involved in such an enterprise. The reader must not forget that Thoreau wrote prospectively, not of what he had done, or of what he was, but of what, being the man he was, he felt he ought to do. While *Walden* itself was written only after his sojourn by the pond had ended, it grew directly from Thoreau's observations and experiences there. The writing of *Walden* was the next experiment in the series.

Overall, the point of view of the unbound observer best suited Thoreau. He did not refrain from participating in politics, in commerce, from involving himself with Concord or addressing the society at large, but he did so always with an eye for his freedom, leaving the door ajar. Freedom, for Thoreau, meant being able to come and go from society at will, not conforming but cooperating when he felt it right to do so, without being bound to cooperate forever after. Nature and society are each refuges from the other. The knowledge that, in each place, one has a reserve in the other is a source of confidence. So Thoreau did not scruple to dine with the Emersons or with his mother during his sojourn in the woods, nor did he force himself to remain in town when it became oppressive, but returned to his shanty by the pond.

So—and this must be stated clearly—*Walden* is not an exercise in self-aggrandizement, a deliberately-crafted legend Thoreau spun about himself, but a prospectus of an extended program of self-improvement, notes made while already underway. To take Thoreau to task for having failed the ideal of a life of principle is plainly to misunderstand the concept of a principled life. Thoreau's was the very model of a principled life.

Whether or not it is responsible to withdraw from society begs the question whether or not misrepresentation of the self, merely for the sake of expedience, is not a worse withdrawal. An individual who does not know himself, his own worth, and his own freedom, may not cooperate freely. Unless one is constantly mindful of the bases of life, one is not truly able to represent oneself properly in society—better to avoid mankind and deal with society only when one has something of one's own to contribute than to live among humanity all the time and become a false and hollow shell. Giving a false self is worse than giving nothing at all.

Likewise, it is better to get into occasional trouble as a consequence of stubborn insistence upon your own judgment, if it means that on other occasions you are able to give something uniquely your own, than to substitute a blank for yourself. One must fulfill one's responsibilities first to oneself, to become free, before one can freely respond to others, and therefore be socially responsible. In all aspects, this is the task of freedom.

> There is an incessant influx of novelty into the world, and yet we tolerate an incredible dulness [sic]. I need only suggest what kind of sermons are still listened to in the most enlightened countries. There are such words as joy and sorrow, but they are only the burden of a psalm, sung with a nasal twang, while we believe in the ordinary and mean. We think that we can change our clothes only. It is said that the British Empire is very large and respectable, and that the United States are a first-rate power. We do not believe that a tide rises and falls behind every man which can float the British Empire like a chip, if he should ever harbor it in his mind. Who knows what sort of seventeen-year locust will next come out of the ground? The government of the world I live in was not framed, like that of Britain, in after-dinner conversations over the wine. (*Walden*, 586-587)

An object-lesson: when Thoreau chose to involve himself in his father's pencil-making business, he introduced specific refinements into the manufacturing process, particularly of the graphite itself, which resulted in the first American-made pencils good enough to compete with the European product. As a direct consequence of these innovations, the Thoreau family was in time able to give up the manufacture of pencils to become wholesale graphite vendors—a more lucrative business. Thoreau himself wanted no further part of it. Having made his contributions to the family industry in the space of a few months, Thoreau simply replaced his hat on his head and returned, with his notebook, to the woods.

RALPH WALDO EMERSON

Thoreau

[1862]

*When Thoreau died in 1862, his friend and neighbor Ralph Waldo
Emerson was asked to preach the funeral sermon. This eulogy was
later revised and published as an essay. Perhaps no other single
work had such a wide influence on the reputation of Thoreau.
Written with every intention of honoring a departed friend, it had
a most devastating effect on his fame. Emerson idealized Thoreau
as a Stoic. When he came to edit Thoreau's letters in 1865, he cut
from them every line that showed his warm, friendly personality,
and emphasized his philosophical aloofness. The same touch can be
discerned here. Thoreau is portrayed essentially in the negative, as
one who found it easier to say No than Yes. Emerson created the
concept of Thoreau as an unfeeling Stoic. Paradoxically enough, it
was Emerson's son Edward who later most emphatically protested
this picture of Thoreau and who helped in his centennial tribute,*
Henry Thoreau as Remembered by a Young Friend, *to
rehabilitate him as the most vital of all the Transcendentalists.*
—Walter Harding

From *Thoreau: A Century of Criticism*, Walter Harding, ed.: pp. 22-40 (Southern Methodist
University Press, 1954). © 1954 by Southern Methodist University Press. Reprinted by
permission.

Henry David Thoreau was the last male descendant of a French ancestor who came to this country from the Isle of Guernsey. His character exhibited occasional traits drawn from this blood, in singular combination with a very strong Saxon genius.

He was born in Concord, Massachusetts, on the 12th of July, 1817. He was graduated at Harvard College in 1837, but without any literary distinction. An iconoclast in literature, he seldom thanked colleges for their service to him, holding them in small esteem, whilst yet his debt to them was important. After leaving the University, he joined his brother in teaching a private school, which he soon renounced. His father was a manufacturer of lead-pencils, and Henry applied himself for a time to this craft, believing he could make a better pencil than was in use then. After completing his experiments, he exhibited his work to chemists and artists in Boston, and having obtained their certificates to its excellence and to its equality with the best London manufacture, he returned home contented. His friends congratulated him that he had now opened his way to fortune. But he replied, that he should never make another pencil. "Why should I? I would not do again what I have done once." He resumed his endless walks and miscellaneous studies, making every day some new acquaintance with Nature, though as yet never speaking of zoology or botany, since, though very studious of natural facts, he was incurious of technical and textual science.

At this time, a strong, healthy youth, fresh from college, whilst all his companions were choosing their profession, or eager to begin some lucrative employment, it was inevitable that his thoughts should be exercised on the same question, and it required rare decision to refuse all the accustomed paths and keep his solitary freedom at the cost of disappointing the natural expectations of his family and friends: all the more difficult that he had a perfect probity, was exact in securing his own independence, and in holding every man to the like duty. But Thoreau never faltered. He was a born protestant. He declined to give up his large ambition of knowledge and action for any narrow craft or profession, aiming at a much more comprehensive calling, the art of living well. If he slighted and defied the opinions of others, it was only that he was more intent to reconcile his practice with his own belief. Never idle or self-indulgent, he preferred, when he wanted money, earning it by some piece of manual labor agreeable to him, as building a boat or a fence, planting, grafting, surveying, or other short work, to any long engagements. With his hardy habits and few wants, his skill in wood-craft, and his powerful arithmetic, he was very competent to live in any part of the world. It would cost him less time to supply his wants than another. He was therefore secure of his leisure.

A natural skill for mensuration, growing out of his mathematical knowledge and his habit of ascertaining the measures and distances of objects which interested him, the size of trees, the depth and extent of ponds and rivers, the height of mountains, and the air-line distance of his favorite summits,—this, and his intimate knowledge of the territory about Concord, made him drift into the profession of land-surveyor. It had the advantage for him that it led him continually into new and secluded grounds, and helped his studies of Nature. His accuracy and skill in this work were readily appreciated, and he found all the employment he wanted.

He could easily solve the problems of the surveyor, but he was daily beset with graver questions, which he manfully confronted. He interrogated every custom, and wished to settle all his practice on an ideal foundation. He was a Protestant *á outrance*, and few lives contain so many renunciations. He was bred to no profession; he never married; he lived alone; he never went to church; he never voted; he refused to pay a tax to the State; he ate no flesh, he drank no wine, he never knew the use of tobacco; and, though a naturalist, he used neither trap nor gun. He chose, wisely no doubt, for himself, to be the bachelor of thought and Nature. He had no talent for wealth, and knew how to be poor without the least hint of squalor or inelegance. Perhaps he fell into his way of living without forecasting it much, but approved it with later wisdom. "I am often reminded," he wrote in his journal, "that if I had bestowed on me the wealth of Croesus, my aims must be still the same, and my means essentially the same." He had no temptations to fight against,—no appetites, no passions, no taste for elegant trifles. A fine house, dress, the manners and talk of highly cultivated people were all thrown away on him. He much preferred a good Indian, and considered these refinements as impediments to conversation, wishing to meet his companion on the simplest terms. He declined invitations to dinner-parties, because there each was in every one's way, and he could not meet the individuals to any purpose. "They make their pride," he said, "in making their dinner cost much; I make my pride in making my dinner cost little." When asked at table what dish he preferred, he answered,

"The nearest." He did not like the taste of wine, and never had a vice in his life. He said,—"I have a faint recollection of pleasure derived from smoking dried lily-stems, before I was a man. I had commonly a supply of these. I have never smoked anything more noxious."

He chose to be rich by making his wants few, and supplying them himself. In his travels, he used the railroad only to get over so much country as was unimportant to the present purpose, walking hundreds of miles, avoiding taverns, buying a lodging in farmers' and fishermen's houses, as cheaper, and more agreeable to him, and because there he could better find the men and the information he wanted.

There was somewhat military in his nature, not to be subdued, always manly and able, but rarely tender, as if he did not feel himself except in opposition. He wanted a fallacy to expose, a blunder to pillory, I may say required a little sense of victory, a roll of the drum, to call his powers into full exercise. It cost him nothing to say No; indeed he found it much easier than to say Yes. It seemed as if his first instinct on hearing a proposition was to controvert it, so impatient was he of the limitations of our daily thought. This habit, of course, is a little chilling to the social affections; and though the companion would in the end acquit him of any malice or untruth, yet it mars conversation. Hence, no equal companion stood in affectionate relations with one so pure and guileless. "I love Henry," said one of his friends, "but I cannot like him; and as for taking his arm, I should as soon think of taking the arm of an elm-tree."

Yet, hermit and stoic as he was, he was really fond of sympathy, and threw himself heartily and childlike into the company of young people whom he loved, and whom he delighted to entertain, as he only could, with the varied and endless anecdotes of his experiences by field and river: and he was always ready to lead a huckleberry-party or a search for chestnuts or grapes. Talking, one day, of a public discourse, Henry remarked, that whatever succeeded with the audience was bad. I said, "Who would not like to write something which all can read, like Robinson Crusoe? and who does not see with regret that his page is not solid with a right materialistic treatment, which delights everybody?" Henry objected, of course, and vaunted the better lectures which reached only a few persons. But, at supper, a young girl, understanding that he was to lecture at the Lyceum, sharply asked him, "Whether his lecture would be a nice, interesting story, such as she wished to hear, or whether it was one of those old philosophical things that she did not care about." Henry turned to her, and bethought himself, and, I saw, was trying to believe that he had matter that might fit her and her brother who were to sit up and go to the lecture, if it was a good one for them.

He was a speaker and actor of the truth, born such, and was ever running into dramatic situations from this cause. In any circumstance it interested all bystanders to know what part Henry would take, and what he would say; and he did not disappoint expectation, but used an original judgment on each emergency. In 1845 he built himself a small framed house on the shores of Walden Pond, and lived there two years alone, a life of labor and study. This action was quite native and fit for him. No one who knew him would tax him with affectation. He was more unlike his neighbors in his thought than in his action. As soon as he had exhausted the advantages of that solitude, he abandoned it. In 1847, not approving some uses to which the public expenditure was applied, he refused to pay his town tax, and was put in jail. A friend paid the tax for him, and he was released. The like annoyance was threatened the next year. But, as his friends paid the tax, notwithstanding his protest, I believe he ceased to resist. No opposition or ridicule had any weight with him. He coldly and fully stated his opinion without affecting to believe that it was the opinion of the company. It was of no consequence if every one present held the opposite opinion. On one occasion he went to the University Library to procure some books. The librarian refused to lend them. Mr. Thoreau repaired to the President, who stated to him the rules and usages, which permitted the loan of books to resident graduates, to clergymen who were alumni, and to some others resident within a circle of ten miles' radius from the College. Mr. Thoreau explained to the President that the railroad had destroyed the old scale of distances,—that the library was useless, yes, and President and College useless, on the terms of his rules,—that the one benefit be owed to the College was its library,—that, at this moment, not only his want of books was imperative but he wanted a large number of books, and assured him that he, Thoreau, and not the librarian, was the proper custodian of these. In short, the President found the petitioner so formidable, and the rules getting to look so ridiculous, that he ended by giving him a privilege which in his hands proved unlimited thereafter.

No truer American existed than Thoreau. His preference of his country and condition was genuine, and his aversation from English and European manners and tastes almost reached contempt. He listened impatiently to news or *bonmots* gleaned from London circles; and though he tried to be civil, these anecdotes fatigued him. The men were all imitating each other, and on a small mould. Why can they not live as far apart as possible, and each be a man by himself? What he sought was the most energetic nature; and he wished to go to Oregon, not to London. "In every part of Great Britain," he wrote in his diary, "are discovered traces of the Romans, their funereal urns, their camps, their roads, their dwellings. But New England, at least, is not based on any Roman ruins. We have not to lay the foundations of our houses on the ashes of a former civilization."

But, idealist as he was, standing for abolition of slavery, abolition of tariffs, almost for abolition of government, it is needless to say he found himself not only unrepresented in actual politics, but almost equally opposed to every class of reformers. Yet he paid the tribute of his uniform respect to the Anti-Slavery party. One man, whose personal acquaintance he had formed, he honored with exceptional regard. Before the first friendly word had been spoken for Captain John Brown, be sent notices to most houses in Concord that he would speak in a public hall on the condition and character of John Brown, on Sunday evening, and invited all people to come. The Republican Committee, the Abolitionist Committee, sent him word that it was premature and not advisable. He replied,—"I did not send to you for advice, but to announce that I am to speak." The hall was filled at an early hour by people of all parties, and his earnest eulogy of the hero was heard by all respectfuly, by many with a sympathy that surprised themselves.

It was said of Plotinus that he was ashamed of his body, and 'tis very likely he had good reason for it,—that his body was a bad servant, and he had not skill in dealing with the material world, as happens often to men of abstract intellect. But Mr. Thoreau was equipped with a most adapted and serviceable body. He was of short stature, firmly built, of light complexion, with strong, serious blue eyes, and a grave aspect,—his face covered in the late years with a becoming beard. His senses were acute, his frame well-knit and hardy, his hands strong and skillful in the use of tools. And there was a wonderful fitness of body and mind. He could pace sixteen rods more accurately than another man could measure them with rod and chain. He could find his path in the woods at night, he said, better by his feet than his eyes. He could estimate the measure of a tree very well by his eye; he could estimate the weight of a calf or a pig, like a dealer. From a box containing a bushel or more of loose pencils, he could take up with his hands fast enough just a dozen pencils at every grasp. He was a good swimmer, runner, skater, boatman, and would probably outwalk most countrymen in a day's journey. And the relation of body to mind was still finer than we have indicated. He said he wanted every stride his legs made. The length of his walk uniformly made the length of his writing. If shut up in the house, he did not write at all.

He had a strong common-sense, like that which Rose Flammock the weaver's daughter in Scott's romance commends in her father, as resembling a yardstick, which, whilst it measures dowlas and diaper, can equally well measure tapestry and cloth of gold. He had always a new resource. When I was planting forest trees, and had procured half a peck of acorns, he said that only a small portion of them would be sound, and proceeded to examine them and select the sound ones. But finding this took time, he said, "I think if you put them all into water the good ones will sink;" which experiment we tried with success. He could plan a garden or a house or a barn; would have been competent to lead a "Pacific Exploring Expedition;" could give judicious counsel in the gravest private or public affairs.

He lived for the day, not cumbered and mortified by his memory. If he brought you yesterday a new proposition, he would bring you today another not less revolutionary. A very industrious man, and setting, like all highly organized men, a high value on his time, he seemed the only man of leisure in town, always ready for any excursion that promised well, or for conversation prolonged into late hours. His trenchant sense was never stopped by his rules of daily prudence, but was always up to the new occasion. He liked and used the simplest food, yet, when some one urged a vegetable diet, Thoreau thought all diets a very small matter, saying that "the man who shoots the buffalo lives better than the man who boards at the Graham House." He said,—"You can sleep near the railroad, and never be disturbed: Nature knows very well what sounds are worth attending to, and has made up her mind not to hear the railroad-whistle. But things respect the devout mind, and a mental ecstasy was never interrupted." He noted what repeatedly befell him, that, after receiving from a distance a rare plant, he would presently find the same in his own haunts. And those pieces of luck which happen only to good players happened to him. One day, walking with a stranger, who inquired where Indian arrow-heads could be found, he replied, "Everywhere," and, stooping forward, picked one on the instant from the ground. At Mount Washington, in Tuckerman's Ravine, Thoreau had a bad fall, and sprained his foot. As he was in the act of getting up from his fall, he saw for the first time the leaves of the *Arnica mollis.*

His robust common sense, armed with stout hands, keen perceptions and strong will, cannot yet account for the superiority which shone in his simple and hidden life. I must add the cardinal fact, that there was an excellent wisdom in him, proper to a rare class of men, which showed him the material world as a means and symbol. This discovery, which sometimes yields to poets a certain casual and interrupted light, serving for the ornament of their writing, was in him an unsleeping insight; and whatever faults or obstructions of temperament might cloud it, he was not disobedient to the heavenly vision. In his youth, he said, one day, "The other world is all my art; my pencils will draw no other; my jackknife will cut nothing else; I do not use it as a means." This was the muse and genius that ruled his opinions, conversation, studies, work and course of life. This made him a searching judge of men. At first glance he measured his companion, and, though insensible to some fine traits of culture, could very well report his weight and calibre. And this made the impression of genius which his conversation sometimes gave.

He understood the matter in hand at a glance, and saw the limitations and poverty of those he talked with, so that nothing seemed concealed from such terrible eyes. I have repeatedly known young men of sensibility converted in a moment to the belief that this was the man they were in search of, the man of men, who could tell them all they should do. His own dealing with them was never affectionate, but superior, didactic, scorning their petty ways,—very slowly conceding, or not conceding at all, the promise of his society at their houses, or even at his own. "Would he not walk with them?" "He did not know. There was nothing so important to him as his walk; he had no walks to throw away on company." Visits were offered him from respectful parties, but he declined them. Admiring friends offered to carry him at their own cost to the Yellowstone River,—to the West Indies,—to South America. But though nothing could be more grave or considered than his refusals, they remind one, in quite new relations, of that fop Brummell's reply to the gentleman who offered him his carriage in a shower, "But where will you ride, then?"—and what accusing silences, and what searching and irresistible speeches, battering down all defenses, his companions can remember!

Mr. Thoreau dedicated his genius with such entire love to the fields, hills and waters of his native town, that he made them known and interesting to all reading Americans, and to people over the sea. The river on whose banks he was born and died he knew from its springs to its confluence with the Merrimack. He had made summer and winter observations on it for many years, and at every hour of the day and night. The result of the recent survey of the Water Commissioners appointed by the State of Massachusetts he had reached by his private experiments, several years earlier. Every fact which occurs in the bed, on the banks, or in the air over it; the fishes, and their spawning and nests, their manners, their food; the shad-flies which fill the air on a certain evening once a year, and which are snapped at by the fishes so ravenously that many of these die of repletion; the conical heaps of small stones on the river-shallows, the huge nests of small fishes, one of which will sometimes overfill a cart; the birds which frequent the stream, heron, duck, sheldrake, loon, osprey; the snake, muskrat, otter, woodchuck and fox, on the banks; the turtle, frog, hyla, and cricket; which make the banks vocal,—were all known to him, and, as it were, townsmen and fellow—creatures; so that he felt an absurdity or violence in any narrative of one of these by itself apart, and still more of its dimensions on an inch-rule, or in the exhibition of its skeleton, or the specimen of a squirrel or a bird in brandy. He liked to speak of the manners of the river, as itself a lawful creature, yet with exactness, and always to an observed fact. As he knew the river, so the ponds in this region.

One of the weapons he used, more important to him than microscope or alcohol-receiver to other investigators, was a whim which grew on him by indulgence, yet appeared in gravest statement, namely, of extolling his own town and neighborhood as the most favored centre for natural observation. He remarked that the Flora of Massachusetts embraced almost all the important plants of America,—most of the oaks, most of the willows, the best pines, the ash, the maple, the beech, the nuts. He returned Kane's "Arctic Voyage" to a friend of whom he had borrowed it, with the remark, that "Most of the phenomena noted might be observed in Concord." He seemed a little envious of the Pole, for the coincident sunrise and sunset, or five minutes' day after six months: a splendid fact, which Annursnuc had never afforded him. He found red snow in one of his walks, and told me that he expected to find yet the *Victoria regia* in Concord. He was the attorney of the indigenous plants, and owned to a preference of the weeds to the imported plants as of the Indian to the civilized man, and noticed, with pleasure, that the willow bean-poles of his neighbor had grown more than his beans. "See these weeds," he said, "which have been hoed at by a million farmers all spring and summer, and yet have prevailed, and just now come out triumphant over all lanes, pastures, fields and gardens, such is their vigor. We have insulted them with low names, too,—as Pigweed, Wormwood, Chickweed, Shad-blossom." He says, "They have brave names, too,— Ambrosia, Stellaria, Amelanchier, Amaranth, etc."

I think his fancy for referring everything to the meridian of Concord did not grow out of any ignorance or depreciation of other longitudes or latitudes, but was rather a playful expression of his conviction of the indifferency of all places, and that the best place for each is where he stands. He expressed it once in this wise:—"I think nothing is to be hoped from you, if this bit of mould under your feet is not sweeter to you to eat than any other in this world, or in any world."

The other weapon with which he conquered all obstacles in science was patience. He knew how to sit immovable, a part of the rock he rested on, until the bird, the reptile, the fish, which had retired from him, should come back and resume its habits, nay, moved by curiosity, should come to him and watch him.

It was a pleasure and a privilege to walk with him. He knew the country like a fox or a bird, and passed through it as freely by paths of his own. He knew every track in the snow or on the ground, and what creature had taken this path before him. One must submit abjectly to such a guide, and the reward was great. Under his arm he carried an old music-book to press plants; in his pocket, his diary and pencil, a spy-glass for birds, microscope, jack-knife, and twine. He wore a straw hat, stout shoes, strong gray trousers, to brave scrub-oaks and smilax, and to climb a tree for a hawk's or a squirrel's nest. He waded into the pool for the water-plants, and his strong legs were no insignificant part of his armor. On the day I speak of he looked for the Menyanthes, detected it across the wide pool, and, on examination of the florets, decided that it had been in flower five days. He drew out of his breast-pocket his diary, and read the names of all the plants that should bloom on this day, whereof he kept account as a banker when his notes fall due. The Cypripedium not due till to-morrow. He thought that, if waked up from a trance, in this swamp, he could tell by the plants what time of the year it was within two days. The redstart was flying about, and presently the fine grosbeaks, whose brilliant scarlet "makes the rash gazer wipe his eye," and whose fine clear note Thoreau compared to that of a tanager which has got rid of its hoarseness. Presently he heard a note which he called that of the night-warbler, a bird he had never identified, had been in search of twelve years, which always, when he saw it was in the act of diving down into a tree or bush, and which it was vain to seek; the only bird which sings indifferently by night and by day. I told him he must beware of finding and booking it, lest life should have nothing more to show him. He said, "What you seek in vain for, half your life, one day you come full upon, all the family at dinner. You seek it like a dream, and as soon as you find it you become its prey."

His interest in the flower or the bird lay very deep in his mind, was connected with Nature,—and the meaning of Nature was never attempted to be defined by him. He would not offer a memoir of his observations to the Natural History Society. "Why should I? To detach the description from its connections in my mind would make it no longer true or valuable to me: and they do not wish what belongs to it." His power of observation seemed to indicate additional senses. He saw as with microscope, heard as with ear-trumpet, and his memory was a photographic register of all he saw and heard. And yet none knew better than he that it is not the fact that imports, but the impression or effect of the fact on your mind. Every fact lay in glory in his mind, a type of the order and beauty of the whole.

His determination on Natural History was organic. He confessed that he sometimes felt like a hound or a panther, and, if born among Indians, would have been a fell hunter. But, restrained by his Massachusetts culture, he played out the game in this mild form of botany and ichthyology. His intimacy with animals suggested what Thomas Fuller records of Butler the apiologist, that "either he had told the bees things or the bees had told him." Snakes coiled round his leg; the fishes swam into his hand, and he took them out of the water; he pulled the woodchuck out of its hole by the tail and took the foxes under his protection from the hunters. Our naturalist had perfect magnanimity; he had no secrets: he would carry you to the heron's haunt, or even to his most prized botanical swamp,—possibly knowing that you could never find it again, yet willing to take his risks.

No college ever offered him a diploma, or a professor's chair; no academy made him its corresponding secretary, its discoverer, or even its member. Perhaps these learned bodies feared the satire of his presence. Yet so much knowledge of Nature's secret and genius few others possessed; none in a more large and religious synthesis. For not a particle of respect had he to the opinions of any man or body of men, but homage solely to the truth itself; and as he discovered everywhere among doctors some leaning of courtesy, it discredited them. He grew to be revered and admired by his townsmen, who had at first known him only as an oddity. The farmers who employed him as a surveyor soon discovered his rare accuracy and skill, his knowledge of their lands, of trees, of birds, of Indian remains and the like, which enabled him to tell every farmer more than he knew before of his own farm; so that he began to feel a little as if Mr. Thoreau had better rights in his land than he. They felt, too, the superiority of character which addressed all men with a native authority.

Indian relics abound in Concord,—arrow-heads, stone chisels, pestles, and fragments of pottery; and on the river-bank, large heaps of clam-shells and ashes mark spots which the savages frequented. These, and every circumstance touching the Indian, were important in his eyes. His visits to Maine were chiefly for love of the Indian. He had the satisfaction of seeing the manufacture of the bark-canoe, as well as of trying his hand in its management on the rapids. He was inquisitive about the making of the stone arrow-head, and in his last days charged a youth setting out for the Rocky Mountains to find an Indian who could tell him that: "It was well worth a visit to California to learn it." Occasionally, a small party of Penobscot Indians would visit Concord, and pitch their tents for a few weeks in summer on the river-bank. He failed not to make acquaintance with the best of them; though he well knew that asking questions of Indians is like catechizing beavers and rabbits. In his last visit to Maine he had great satisfaction from Joseph Polis, an intelligent Indian of Oldtown, who was his guide for some weeks.

He was equally interested in every natural fact. The depth of his perception found likeness of law throughout Nature, and I know not any genius who so swiftly inferred universal law from the single fact. He was no pedant of a department. His eye was open to beauty, and his ear to music. He found these, not in rare conditions, but wheresoever he went. He thought the best of music was in single strains; and he found poetic suggestion in the humming of the telegraph-wire.

His poetry might be bad or good; he no doubt wanted a lyric facility and technical skill, but he had the source of poetry in his spiritual perception. He was a good reader and critic, and his judgment on poetry was to the ground of it. He could not be deceived as to the presence or absence of the poetic element in any composition, and his thirst for this made him negligent and perhaps scornful of superficial graces. He would pass by many delicate rhythms, but he would have detected every live stanza or line in a volume, and knew very well where to find an equal poetic charm in prose. He was so enamored of the spiritual beauty that he held all actual written poems in very light esteem in the comparison. He admired Æschylus and Pindar; but, when some one was commending them, he said that Æschylus and the Greeks, in describing Apollo and Orpheus, had given no song, or no good one. "They ought not to have moved trees, but to have chanted to the gods such a hymn as would have sung all their old ideas out of their heads, and new ones in." His own verses are often rude and defective. The gold does not yet run pure, is drossy and crude. The thyme and marjoram are not yet honey. But if he want lyric fineness and technical merits, if he have not the poetic temperament, he never lacks the casual thought, showing that his genius was better than his talent. He knew the worth of the Imagination for the uplifting and consolation of human life, and liked to throw every thought into a symbol. The fact you tell is of no value, but only the impression. For this reason his presence was poetic, always piqued the curiosity to know more deeply the secrets of his mind. He had many reserves, an unwillingness to exhibit to profane eyes what was still sacred in his own, and knew well how to throw a poetic veil over his experience. All readers of "Walden" will remember his mythical record of his disappointments:—

"I long ago lost a hound, a bay horse and a turtle-dove, and am still on their trail. Many are the travellers I have spoken concerning them, describing their tracks, and what calls they answered to. I have met one or two who have heard the hound, and the tramp of the horse, and even seen the dove disappear behind a cloud; and they seemed as anxious to recover them as if they had lost them them-selves."

His riddles were worth the reading, and I confide that if at any time I do not understand the expression, it is yet just. Such was the wealth of his truth that it was not worth his while to use words in vain. His poem entitled "Sympathy" reveals the tenderness under that triple steel of stoicism, and the intellectual subtility it could animate. His classic poem on "Smoke" suggests Simonides, but is better than any poem of Simonides. His biography is in his verses. His habitual thought makes all his poetry a hymn to the Cause of causes, the Spirit which vivifies and controls his own:—

> "I hearing get, who had but ears,
> And sight, who had but eyes before;
> I moments live, who lived but years,
> And truth discern, who knew but learning's lore."

And still more in these religious lines:—

> "Now chiefly is my natal hour
> And only now my prime of life;
> I will not doubt the love untold,
> Which not my worth nor want have bought,
> Which wooed me young, and wooes me old,
> And to this evening hath me brought."

Whilst he used in his writings a certain petulance of remark in reference to churches or churchmen, he was a person of a rare, tender and absolute religion, a person incapable of any profanation, by act or by thought. Of course, the same isolation which belonged to his original thinking and living detached him from the social religious forms. This is neither to be censured nor regretted. Aristotle long ago explained it, when he said, "One who surpasses his fellow-citizens in virtue is no longer a part of the city. Their law is not for him, since he is a law to himself."

Thoreau was sincerity itself, and might fortify the convictions of prophets in the ethical laws by his holy living. It was an affirmative experience which refused to be set aside. A truth-speaker he, capable of the most deep and strict conversation; a physician to the wounds of any soul; a friend, knowing not only the secret of friendship, but almost worshipped by those few persons who resorted to him as their confessor and prophet, and knew the deep value of his mind and great heart. He thought that without religion or devotion of some kind nothing great was ever accomplished: and he thought that the bigoted sectarian had better bear this in mind.

His virtues, of course, sometimes ran into extremes. It was easy to trace to the inexorable demand on all for exact truth that austerity which made this willing hermit more solitary even than he wished. Himself of a perfect probity, he required not less of others. He had a disgust at crime, and no worldly success would cover it. He detected paltering as readily in dignified and prosperous persons as in beggars, and with equal scorn. Such dangerous frankness was in his dealing that his admirers called him "that terrible Thoreau," as if he spoke when silent, and was still present when he had departed. I think the severity of his ideal interfered to deprive him of a healthy sufficiency of human society.

The habit of a realist to find things the reverse of their appearance inclined him to put every statement in a paradox. A certain habit of antagonism defaced his earlier writings,—a trick of rhetoric not quite outgrown in his later, of substituting for the obvious word and thought its diametrical opposite. He praised wild mountains and winter forests for their domestic air, in snow and ice he would find sultriness, and commended the wilderness for resembling Rome and Paris. "It was so dry, that you might call it wet."

The tendency to magnify the moment, to read all the laws of Nature in the one object or one combination under your eye, is of course comic to those who do not share the philosopher's perception of identity. To him there was no such thing as size. The pond was a small ocean; the Atlantic, a large Walden Pond. He referred every minute fact to cosmical laws. Though he meant to be just, he seemed haunted by a certain chronic assumption that the science of the day pretended completeness, and he had just found out that the *savans* had neglected to discriminate a particular botanical variety, had failed to describe the seeds or count the sepals. "That is to say," we replied, "the blockheads were not born in Concord; but who said they were? It was their unspeakable misfortune to be born in London, or Paris, or Rome; but, poor fellows, they did what they could, considering that they never saw Bateman's Pond, or Nine-Acre Corner, or Becky Stow's Swamp; besides, what were you sent into the world for, but to add this observation?"

Had his genius been only contemplative, he had been fitted to his life, but with his energy and practical ability he seemed born for great enterprise and for command; and I so much regret the loss of his rare powers of action, that I cannot help counting it a fault in him that he had no ambition. Wanting this, instead of engineering for all America, he was the captain of a huckleberry-party. Pounding beans is good to the end of pounding empires one of these days; but if, at the end of years, it is still only beans!

But these foibles, real or apparent, were fast vanishing in the incessant growth of a spirit so robust and wise, and which effaced its defeats with new triumphs. His study of Nature was a perpetual ornament to him, and inspired his friends with curiosity to see the world through his eyes, and to hear his adventures. They possessed every kind of interest.

He had many elegancies of his own, whilst he scoffed at conventional elegance. Thus, he could not bear to hear the sound of his own steps, the grit of gravel; and therefore never willingly walked in the road, but in the grass, on mountains and in woods. His senses were acute, and he remarked that by night every dwelling-house gives out bad air, like a slaughter-house. He liked the pure fragrance of melilot. He honored certain plants with special regard, and, over all, the pond-lily,— then, the gentian, and the *Mikania scandens*, and "life-everlasting," and a bass-tree which he visited every year when it bloomed, in the middle of July. He thought the scent a more oracular inquisition than the sight,— more oracular and trustworthy. The scent, of course, reveals what is concealed from the other senses. By it he detected earthiness. He delighted in echoes, and said they were almost the only kind of kindred voices that he heard. He loved Nature so well, was so happy in her solitude, that he became very jealous of cities, the sad work which their refinements and artifices made with man and his dwelling. The axe was always destroying his forest. "Thank God," he said, "they cannot cut down the clouds!" "All kinds of figures are drawn on the blue ground with this fibrous white paint...."

There is a flower known to botanists, one of the same genus with our summer plant called "Life-Everlasting," a *Gnaphalium* like that, which grows on the most inaccessible cliffs of the Tyrolese mountains, where the chamois dare hardly venture, and which the hunter, tempted by its beauty, and by his love (for it is immensely valued by the Swiss maidens), climbs the cliffs to gather, and is sometimes found dead at the foot, with the flower in his hand. It is called by botanists the *Gnaphalium leontopodium*, but by the Swiss *Edelweisse*, which signifies *Noble Purity*. Thoreau seemed to me living in the hope to gather this plant, which belonged to him of right. The scale on which his studies proceeded was so large as to require longevity, and we were the less prepared for his sudden disappearance. The country knows not yet, or in the least part, how great a son it has lost. It seems an injury that he should leave in the midst his broken task which none else can finish, a kind of indignity to so noble a soul that he should depart out of Nature before yet he has been really shown to his peers for what he is. But he, at least, is content. His soul was made for the noblest society; he had in a short life exhausted the capabilities of this world; wherever there is knowledge, wherever there is virtue, wherever there is beauty, he will find a home.

NOTE

* From *Atlantic Monthly*, X (August, 1862), 239–49. A long series of quotations has been omitted.

WALTER HARDING

Thoreau's Ideas

Before any attempt can be made to examine Thoreau's philosophy and present an organized analysis of his ideas, it is important to recognize that he never made any such attempt himself. "Thoreau will remain forever baffling if we insist on resolving into perfect harmony all his ideas and impulses, since there is every reason to believe he did not himself harmonize them" (Foerster, *Nature in American Literature*, p. 119). Thoreau, like most of the other Transcendentalists, was essentially an eclectic. He picked up his ideas from hither and yon, accepting what interested him and ignoring the rest. As he grew older, many of his ideas inevitably changed, but that did not disturb him. In any one period of his life he was usually consistent. Contradictions can be found only if one places in juxtaposition statements Thoreau made at wide intervals of time. Unfortunately there is not space in a brief treatment such as this to indicate in any detail the development of his thought and his changes of attitude. There is a real need for a detailed study devoted to that subject. But until that study is made, we shall have to be content with attempting to understand his most prevalent or most familiar ideas.

Although this problem does raise a serious obstacle to presenting accurately Thoreau's ideas per se, it does offer, on the other hand, an almost unequal opportunity to study the development of a man's mind, since Thoreau's writings, particularly his *Journal*, are so voluminous.

From *A Thoreau Handbook* by Walter Harding: pp. 131-173 (New York University Press, 1959). © 1959 by New York University Press. Reprinted by permission.

"Thoreau's principal achievement was not the creation of a system but the creation of himself, and his principal literary work was, therefore, the presentation of that self in the form of a self-portrait" (Krutch, p. 11). The very fact that Thoreau never crystallized his ideas into a set form, Krutch also suggests, adds immensely to the charm of his writing. Thoreau was always on the search for an answer, and his enthusiasm in that search carries the reader along with him.

But unfortunately altogether too many students of Thoreau have not been willing to accept the fact that Thoreau did not formulate and unify his thinking. Approaching his writings with a preconceived notion that there was a unity to his ideas, they have attempted to impose a consistency where no consistency existed. They have accepted those ideas of his that fitted their own particular orthodoxy and silently rejected the rest. Thus they have been able to "prove" that Thoreau was a stoic or an epicurean, a pacifist or a militarist, a pessimist or an optimist, an individualist or a communist. There is hardly an ism of our times that has not attempted to adopt Thoreau—and yet was there ever a man who so consistently renounced all isms, all preconceived or institutionalized views of the universe?

Perhaps the most popular misconception of Thoreau is that he was a stoic. "He was an ascetic who reveled in self-denial." "He could more easily say no than yes." "He preferred to do without." These are the most frequent reactions to Thoreau. It is easy to discover the basis for this misconception. It was popularized by Ralph Waldo Emerson. Emerson delighted in seeing Thoreau as "the perfect Stoic." It mattered little to him that Thoreau's sister Sophia protested, "Henry never impressed me as the Stoic which Mr. E. represents him" (*Daniel Ricketson and His Friends*, p. 155). To Emerson, Thoreau was a stoic. When he composed Thoreau's funeral address, he overemphasized the negative elements in Thoreau's personality. When he edited Thoreau's *Letters to Various Persons*, he purposely omitted all homely, personal remarks because they did not conform to his preconception. Sophia again protested, this time to the publisher James T. Fields, but Emerson was permitted to have his way. Thus there has been built up in the minds of the people the picture of Thoreau as a stoic, and no amount of evidence to the contrary seems to convince them that their conception is false. I do not wish to imply that Emerson was malicious in his misinterpretation. On the contrary, he was trying his best to emphasize what he thought were Thoreau's greatest values.

Mary Edith Cochnower has examined Thoreau's stoicism at length and has concluded: "He was perhaps as true a Stoic as could have been in his day or any day. He was surprisingly like his ancient prototypes" ("Thoreau and Stoicism," p. 94). But I, for one, feel that she has been highly selective in choosing her evidence and that, as she herself admits, the term "stoicism" has become so broadened and so watered down as to render it virtually meaningless.

F. O. Matthiessen (*American Renaissance*, p. 122) presents the diametrically opposite viewpoint: "In the broad use of the terms, he [Thoreau] is much more of an epicurean than a stoic." It would be foolish to try to epitomize Thoreau's philosophy as "Eat, drink, and be merry, for tomorrow we die." Nothing was much further from his attitude. But if we define (as the dictionary does) an epicurean as one who delights in sensuous pleasure, we do come much closer to certain aspects of Thoreau's outlook. Thoreau was basically sensuous. "See, hear, smell, taste, etc., while these senses are fresh and pure," he says (J, II, 330). When he denied himself sense stimulation—as often he did—it was not through any stoic belief in asceticism for its own sake but through his desire to keep his senses "free and pure" for the higher levels of perception. "I do not take snuff," he says (J, IX, 197). "In my winter walks, I stoop and bruise between my thumb and finger the dry whorls of the lycopus, or water horehound ... and smell that. That is as near as I come to the Spice Islands."

"However much Thoreau wished always to walk in the pure empyrean, he could not check for long his sensuous love for solid earth" (Willson, p. 27). And that sensuous love is obvious throughout his writings. It is because he expresses himself sensuously rather than abstractly that he is so readable. When we read Thoreau at his best, we bring every sense into play. "My body is all sentient," he says. "As I go here or there, I am tickled by this or that I come in contact with, as if touched by the wires of a battery" (J, VIII, 44). And so we the readers see, hear, smell, and taste vicariously through Thoreau. As F. O. Matthiessen has pointed out (*American Renaissance*, p. 87), it is what separates Thoreau most from Emerson and what makes him more readable today. Emerson gives us abstract ideas; Thoreau makes us experience. Perhaps it was because Emerson did not comprehend this difference (maybe it was something beyond his ken) that he misinterpreted Thoreau as a stoic.

But one must be careful not to go too far in depicting Thoreau as an epicurean. He was not interested (theoretically, at least) in sense stimulation for its own sake. It was only a means toward an end. His ultimate goal was to find his place in the universe. He developed his senses to ascertain more accurately where that place was.

Thoreau classified himself as a Transcendentalist. If we use the popular definition that a Transcendentalist is one who believes that one can (and should) go beyond Locke in believing that all knowledge is acquired through the senses, that in order to attain the ultimate in knowledge one must "transcend" the senses, we can unquestionably classify Thoreau as a Transcendentalist. "It is not the invitation which I hear, but which I feel, that I obey," he said at one point (J, II, 181); at another, "My genius makes distinctions which my understanding cannot and which my senses do not report" (J, II, 337). His *Journals*, particularly up to approximately 1850, are filled with avowals of the Transcendental philosophy. The "Higher Laws" chapter of *Walden* is one of his most explicit statements of these beliefs. The account of his reverie on the doorstep of his Walden cabin, which opens the chapter on "Sounds" (W, II, 123–24), is perhaps his best-known account of the Transcendental experience.

But unfortunately as he grew older he found that he was "transcending his senses" less and less frequently, that he was depending more and more on sensuous rather than Transcendental inspiration. Over and over again in his *Journal* of the early 1850's he laments this change: "I fear that the character of my knowledge is from year to year becoming more distinct and scientific; that, in exchange for views as wide as heaven's scope, I am being narrowed down to the field of the microscope. I see details, not wholes nor the shadow of the whole. I count some parts, and say, 'I know'" (J, II, 406).

Thoreau realized that he attained Transcendental insight not through excitement but through serenity. But as the moments of inspiration became fewer and farther between, he paradoxically intensified the search. "What more than anything else brought him out in all weathers—rain, snow, sleet, fog—alone or with a more than superfluous companion, ever and again to the old forest shrines and hillcrest temples, was the mystic's hope of detecting some trace of the Ineffable" (Norman Foerster, *Nature in American Literature*, p. 101). "Ah, those youthful days!" Thoreau lamented, "are they never to return?

when the walker does not too curiously observe particulars, but sees, hears, scents, tastes, and feels only himself,—the phenomena that show themselves in him,—his expanding body, his intellect and heart. No worm or insect, quadruped or bird, confined his view, but the unbounded universe was his. A bird is now become a mote in his eye" (J, V, 75). But the search continued. "The birding and botanizing were not so ill a thing," he rationalized, according to Foerster, "affording just enough occupation—save when they amounted to a tyranny of observation—to prevent his too insistently asking Nature to give him 'a sign.' Even 'the slight distraction of picking berries is favorable,' he found, 'to a mild, abstracted, poetic mood, to sequestered or transcendental thinking'" (*Nature in American Literature*, p. 104).

In Thoreau's later years one will find more and more space in his writings devoted to an external record of nature and less and less to a recounting of Transcendental experiences. It seems at times—and it has led some observers to believe—that in those later years Thoreau abandoned his earlier Transcendentalism for purely scientific observation. But such an interpretation, I believe, is not correct. Never did he completely abandon his belief in the Transcendental approach to knowledge. In his *Journal* for 1856 he wrote: "It is by obeying the suggestions of a higher light within you that you escape from yourself and ... travel totally new paths" (J, IX, 38); in 1858, "In all important crises one can only consult his genius" (J, IX, 379).

It is almost universally agreed that Thoreau is America's greatest nature writer. It was as a nature writer that he first achieved fame, and it is as a nature writer that he is still most widely known.

Thoreau has had a remarkable influence on the development of the natural history essay. Thoreau was "the first of the American writers upon Nature to be concerned with the workmanship of his product" (Hicks, *The Development of the Natural History Essay in American Literature*, p. 88); that is, the first to realize that the natural history essay could be something more than a mere reporting of natural phenomena observed, that it could in fact be a full-fledged type of belles-lettres. He was the first to make the natural history essay "a definite, and separate, literary form as contrasted to the 'Letters' of White and Crèvecœur, the 'Episodes' of Audubon, the 'Rambles' of Godman, and the various 'Journals' and 'Travels' of earlier writers" (Hicks, pp. 88–89). He established the pattern that most nature writers since his day have followed.

But there are certain characteristics of Thoreau's nature writing that neither his predecessors nor his imitators have ever succeeded in duplicating. He gives his readers a unique sense of immediacy. "Most nature writers appear limited, an eye or an ear or a taste or a touch, but in Thoreau the senses are integrated and focussed" (Cook, *Passage to Walden*, p. 51).

Further, Thoreau has a contagious enthusiasm. Up to the moment of his death he succeeded in retaining that sense of wonder and awe in the beauty of the world around him that most of us associate with our childhood. Clifton Fadiman is supposed to have remarked that Thoreau could get more out of ten minutes with a chickadee than most men could get out of a night with Cleopatra. What is even more remarkable, he almost succeeds in convincing us that the chickadee is preferable to Cleopatra.

But the most significant difference between Thoreau and other nature writers is that natural history was never his primary interest. It was always a means toward an end. His basic concern was not with nature itself but with man's place in nature. "It is narrow to be confined to woods and fields and grand aspects of nature only," he says in his *Journal* (J, II, 421). "The greatest and wisest will still be related to men."

Thoreau's greatest scorn, in fact, was directed at those who were "mere accumulators of facts" about nature (J, I, 18). "The anecdotes of science affect me as trivial and petty," he said (*The Moon*, p. 24). He was disturbed that scientists were willing to kill even a snake to ascertain its species. "I feel that this is not the means of acquiring true knowledge" (J, VI, 311). "This haste to kill a bird or a quadruped and make a skeleton of it, which many young men and some old ones exhibit, reminds me of the fable of the man who killed the hen that laid golden eggs, and so got no more gold. It is a perfectly parallel case" (J, XIV, 109). When an ornithologist said to him, "If you hold the bird in your hand ...," he replied, "I would rather hold it in my affections" (J, VI, 253). He was not so much interested in the bird, as "a bird behind the bird,—for a mythology to shine through his ornithology" (Burroughs, *Indoor Studies*, p. 40).

It was this mystical approach that has led many scientists to distrust Thoreau. (Paradoxically, as Willson has pointed out [p. 33], philosophers have distrusted him because he was too scientific.) Havelock Ellis (*The New Spirit*, p. 94) has perhaps been the most vehement in his denunciation of Thoreau's science: "He seems to have been absolutely deficient in scientific sense." Lowell, in his well-known 1865 essay on Thoreau, said, "He discovered nothing. He thought everything a discovery of his own." Bradford Torrey, the editor of Thoreau's *Journal*, thought that he "leaves the present-day reader wondering how so eager a scholar could have spent so many years in learning so comparatively little" (J, I, xliii), and the coeditor of the *Journal*, Francis Allen, in *Thoreau's Bird-Lore*, devoted much space to pointing out Thoreau's errors in ornithology. Fannie Hardy Eckstorm, in her essay on "Thoreau's 'Maine Woods,'" went to some length to emphasize his weakness as a naturalist. W. L. McAtee denounced him as naïve for accepting some of the theories of protective coloration. And even John Burroughs, who, as I have shown above, realized that natural history was not Thoreau's major interest, delighted in disparaging his observations on nature.

Thoreau himself realized that the scientists would not understand his aims. When he was invited by Spencer Fullerton Baird to join the [American] Association for the Advancement of Science, he noted in his *Journal* that he was declining the invitation because "The fact is I am a mystic, a transcendentalist, and a natural philosopher to boot.... I should have told them at once that I was a transcendentalist. That would have been the shortest way of telling them that they would not understand my explanations.... If it had been the secretary of an association of which Plato or Aristotle was the president, I should not have hesitated to describe my studies at once and particularly" (J, V, 4–5).

Thoreau's errors of observation in natural history are not difficult to understand, In the first place, he lacked adequate scientific equipment. He owned no bird glasses at all until 1854, and then he acquired a telescope rather than the far more efficient binoculars. He used his hat as a botany box. And apparently he had to borrow a microscope when he wanted to use one. But he deliberately did without scientific instruments, frequently because he believed they gave a distorted picture of nature. Then too there were few adequate reference books available in his time. Most of the natural history books in his library were British, simply because there were no comparable American counterparts, although he did own Gray's botany, Wilson's ornithology, Harlan's and Audubon's fauna, and Jaeger's entomology, among others.

What was even more important was that American science was still in its most elementary stages. The pioneering work of classification under such men as Agassiz and Gray had just begun. Taxonomy was the major field of science in Thoreau's day. Thoreau was willing to help in laying these important foundations. In the late 1840's he supplied Agassiz himself with many new specimens, including several new fish, a mouse, and more than one tortoise (Charming, p. 264). And he also assisted Thaddeus William Harris in his entomological researches. But taxonomy could never be Thoreau's major interest. He was not so much interested in the individual species as in the interrelation of all species, and particularly in their relation to man. After reporting a new species of fish to the Boston Society of Natural History, he commented: "What is the amount of my discovery to me? It is not that I have got one in a bottle, that it has got a name in a book, but that I have a little fishy friend in the pond" (J, XI, 360). Nearly a century ahead of his time, he was fundamentally an ecologist. He would have had fewer complaints about the narrowness of the scientific view if he could have read some of our twentieth-century ecological studies. And, reciprocally, twentieth-century scientists have begun to realize the values of his broader approach.

Though as an ecologist Thoreau "perhaps never quite attained what could be called real competence in analyzing the relative effects of all of environment," still he "was acutely aware of the complexity of factors which go to make up the living conditions of a plant" (Nash, "Ecology in the Writings of Henry David Thoreau," p. 15). "The remarkable thing about Thoreau's plant ecology is that he *noticed* so complete a list of environmental effects with so little professional guidance" (p. 27). In his ecological studies Thoreau found "a clue to an explanation of the unity and the completeness of nature which [he] had so long accepted in his transcendental faith" (p. 80). "Certainly ecology with its emphasis upon natural law and the study of vital inter-relationships represented the most logical scientific position from which Thoreau could rise to defend his more transcendental convictions as to the greater unities and the essential completeness of Nature" (p. 80).

Thoreau's major specific contribution to science was his discussion of the theory of the succession of forest trees. It is true that his discovery was anticipated by several other scientists. But Thoreau did his work independently, and his essay is still a standard treatise on the subject. Edward Deevey believes that Thoreau was the first American limnologist and that he made an independent discovery of thermal stratification of water. Aldo Leopold has accorded Thoreau the title of "the father of phenology in this country." But Leo Stoller, after extensive study, has concluded that "Thoreau was by no means a pioneer in American phenology and that his observations probably had no part in the development of this aspect of science" (p. 172). And Anna Botsford Comstock, the leader of the nature study movement in American education, has said, "Thoreau is the ideal toward which those of us engaged in nature study have been working" (p. 54).

Since the publication of Thoreau's complete *Journal* in 1906 scientists have come more and more to recognize it as an important source book for studies of American natural history. It was primarily the records available in these books that led Ludlow Griscom to choose the town of Concord as the setting for his study of changing bird populations, *Birds of Concord*. Arthur Bent and Edward Forbush cited Thoreau regularly in their ornithological studies. Dame and Collins used his records in their *Flora of Middlesex County, Massachusetts* (Malden, Mass., 1888), even though the full *Journal* was not available then. I understand that the American Meteorological Society is now combing the *Journal* for early weather records. And the authors of many other natural history textbooks have found his records useful.

In recent years much has been made of the new type of field handbooks in natural history popularized by Roger Tory Peterson. Their primary value is that they epitomize and emphasize the distinctive marks of the various species. It is interesting to discover that a century ago Thoreau called for just such handbooks: "The object should be to describe not those particulars in which a species resembles its genus, for they are many and that would be but a negative description, but those in which it is peculiar, for they are few and positive" (J, V, 189).

But despite Thoreau's insistence that he was not a natural scientist, and apparently quite against his own will, he found himself in the last fifteen years of his life more and more concerned with scientific data for their own sake—a fact well evidenced by the details on the temperature of the water in Walden Pond in *Walden* (W, II, 330–31) and the pages and pages of lists of species in the later *Journal* (many of which were omitted in the printed version). He was quite conscious of this change of attitude and frequently bewailed it with such comments as "I feel I am dissipated by so many observations" (J, V, 45). But he continued increasingly to concern himself with such data. Ironically enough, as I have indicated above, it is just such information that has proved of value to modern scientists. Finally,

> Amateur though he may have remained in any single field, and protester throughout his life that science's perspective was untrustworthy, yet Thoreau's microscope, spy-glass, charts, weather-tables, presses, and collections, his geological surveys, "Zoological Notes," Reports of the Smithsonian Institute, of the Massachusetts [sic] Society of Natural History, of the Massachusetts Agricultural Society, his reading of Audubon, Wilson, Mcgillivray, Bergstein, Littel, and Nuttal, of Loudon, Gray, Harlan, and Lovell, of Fitch, Harris, Kirby, and Spence, of Agassiz and Gould, Abbott, Sowerby, and Chambers, his own field notes and his essays, all attest to the respect and interest which he showed for the natural scientist's acute eye and practice of induction (Christie, p. 81).

There is a widespread confusion as to Thoreau's religious beliefs. When George Ripley reviewed *A Week* for the *New York Tribune*, he denounced Thoreau as a pantheist. I have been told that each spring an elderly lady makes a pilgrimage to Sleepy Hollow Cemetery to place bouquets on the graves of Emerson and Hawthorne and, turning to Thoreau's grave, ends her ceremony by shaking her fist and saying, "None for you, you dirty little atheist." On the other hand, John Sylvester Smith has hailed him as "an American spiritual genius" ("The Philosophic Naturism of Henry David Thoreau," p. 220) and "a man seeking the salvation of his soul" (p. iv). Wherein does the truth lie?

Thoreau never subscribed to any sectarian creed. "We are wont foolishly to think that the creed which a man professes is more significant than the fact he is," he said (J, IX, 144). The Unitarians frequently claim him as one of their own on the basis of the fact that he was baptized by a Unitarian minister and buried from a Unitarian church. But Thoreau specifically renounced membership in the Unitarian Church. When he was invited to deliver a lecture in the basement of an orthodox (that is, Congregational) church, he "trusted he helped to undermine it" (J, IX, 188).

Although he numbered many clergymen among his friends, he disliked ministers in general, complaining that they were men who could not butter their own bread and yet who combined with a thousand like them to "make dipped toast for all eternity" (J, IX, 284). When one clergyman told Thoreau that he was going to dive into his inmost depths, Thoreau replied, "I trust you will not strike your head against the bottom" (J, V, 265). He complained: "The church! it is eminently the timid institution, and the heads and pillars of it are constitutionally and by principle the greatest cowards in the community" (J, XI, 325). He wished that ministers were a little more *dangerous*" (J, XII, 407).

Neither was he interested in homiletics or sectarian theology. In the main, one may say he was uninterested in the deity" (Drake, "A Formal Study of Thoreau," p. 32). Metaphysics, said Channing, was Thoreau's aversion. His more orthodox maiden aunts were exasperated with him because he would take no interest in theological literature and yet found plenty of time to observe frogs (J, V, 58).

Although Thoreau often belittled his own knowledge of the Bible, he was far better read in it than many, perhaps most, professed Christians. It is difficult to read more than a few pages of his writings without finding a biblical quotation or echo. But "he was among the first to see Christian literature as only the purest and most inspiring of the fables about the relation of man to nature and about the infinite capacities of the unaided human spirit" (Lewis, *American Adam*, p. 22).

Thoreau was critical of the effect that religion had upon his contemporaries. He could not see that it made them superior morally to any other race or nation (J, III, 21). In fact, he thought that conversion was often a "blast" upon youth that prevented their full development (J, V, 210). As he grew older he became more and more convinced that the institutionalized churches were a blight on society. Their opposition to abolitionism in particular antagonized him, and in his various antislavery papers he denounced their conservatism roundly.

Yet it is entirely false to think of Thoreau as irreligious. The Rev. John Sylvester Smith recognizes that although Thoreau rejected orthodox theology and dogma,

> He saw what the religious thinkers of his time did not see that their religion was too much indoors, that it was too often a logical and abstract verbalism only, that it possessed a great vocabulary of orthodox thinking and a minimum of classic Christian experience ("The Philosophic Naturism of

Henry David Thoreau," p. 276). [He] held immediate
religious feeling of the aesthetic quality of the world to be
superior, as a means of religious revelation, to scientific
investigation on the one hand and to traditional dogma on
the other (p. 95). Thoreau believed man was meant to
experience God, not to theologize about him.... Thoreau's
"theology" was not a branch of metaphysics, it was an
experience of life (p. 263). Thoreau was seeking for himself
and for his fellowmen ... a fuller and more nearly natural self-
realization, a fulfillment more in harmony with the
constituted quality of man's own being (p. 29).

Unlike some of his fellow Transcendentalists, Thoreau did not
naïvely deny the existence of evil.

His thought does not share in that tendency of typical
American Transcendentalism (of which Emerson is patron
saint) to retreat from experience into the cloud-land glories
of subjective idealism (Smith, p. 112). But it was really only
social and universal maladjustment that he admitted, and not
categorical evil. It was nothing that a good reformation could
not cure (p. 265).

Yet

Thoreau's thinking must be distinguished from that of
Rousseau. The latter held that all social forms corrupt men.
Thoreau held that the organization of society *as he knew it in
his time* was corrupting. He did not despair of social life,
although without question he denounced the value of any
society as being inherently greater than that of the individual
(p. 264). Thoreau's thinking is clear enough. He believed in
God; he believed in man; but he did not believe in
"civilization" as he found it because it is not organized for the
natural and moral good of man (p. 141). For Thoreau,
orientation in nature is not "back to nature" in the
Rousseauistic sense, but rather is it the transcendental idea,
"through nature to God" (p. 182).

Thoreau went to Walden not to escape from civilization but to discover the true civilization that would permit and foster the greatest development of man's spiritual nature.

Finally, Thoreau was interested in a universal religion, an ethical religion that would be based on the high points of all the Bibles of the world. When Moncure Conway, then a student at Harvard Divinity School, told Thoreau he was "studying the Scriptures," Thoreau replied, "Which Scriptures?" He found as much of value in Confucianism, Buddhism, and the other major Oriental religions as in Christianity. One of his important contributions to the *Dial* was his series of selections from these other Bibles, entitled "Ethnical Scriptures." As he said, "To the philosophers, all sects, all nations, are alike. I like Brahma, Hari, Buddha, the Great Spirit, as well as God" (J, II, 4).

From the beginning of his life to the very end, Thoreau believed that all reform must come from within and cannot be imposed by any outside force. We cannot reform society; we can reform only the individual. When each individual reforms himself, then the reformation of society will automatically follow. Reformation through legislation may achieve temporary results, but lasting reformation will be achieved only when each individual convinces himself of its desirability. Such is the basic belief of Transcendentalism. Thoreau was one of the few Transcendentalists to remain true to that belief throughout his life.

Thoreau, in fact, was as suspicious of reformers as a class as he was of clergymen. One of the most amusing passages in his journal is the oft-quoted description of the three reformers who by coincidence landed at his house in Concord at the same time (J, V, 263–65). He thought them "slimy" and did his utmost to make them ill at ease. He questioned their motives and feared that often they were more interested in forwarding their own careers than their reforms. "They cannot tolerate a man who stands by a head above them," he complained (J, V, 365). It is important to remember, however, "though he lacked a wholehearted sympathy for those who advocated far-reaching reforms, Thoreau preferred them vastly to the smug and timid conservatives (Kirchner, "Henry David Thoreau as a Social Critic," p. 237).

Far more than the individual reformers, he mistrusted the reform societies. No matter what their purpose, societies tended to institutionalize themselves. They destroyed rather than developed the strength of the individual:

Speaking of Fourier communities with Bellew, I said that
I suspected any enterprise in which two were engaged
together. "But," said he, "it is difficult to make a stick stand
unless you slant two or more against it." "Oh, no," answered
I, "you may split its lower end to two or three, or drive it
single into the ground, which is the best way; but most men,
when they start on a new enterprise, not only figuratively, but
really, *pull up stakes*. When the sticks prop one another, none,
or only one, stands erect" (J, VII, 500).

Thoreau, said Emerson in "Life and Letters in New England," "was in
his own person a practical answer, almost a refutation to the theories of
the socialists."

Of all the reform movements of his time, the one that came the
closest to leading Thoreau astray from his basic principles of individual
reformation was the abolitionist movement. It was the most vocal, the
most active. Thoreau agreed that slavery was *the* problem of his time. He
spoke out frequently and vociferously against it. He aided Negro slaves
to escape to freedom in Canada. He was one of the first to come to the
defense of John Brown after Harpers Ferry. But never did he officially
join any antislavery movement. And although he wavered at times, I do
not believe he ever completely abandoned his original principles.

Wendell Glick believes differently:

For at least eight years—from 1837 to 1845 ... he
[Thoreau] believed implicitly ... that the reform of society
should be intrusted solely to the forces for good within man
and the universe ("Thoreau and Radical Abolitionism," p.
105). While Thoreau was at Walden Pond, he and his
government had a disagreement [the "Civil Disobedience"
episode] which left its mark and hastened the day of his
willingness to aid radical Abolitionists in their attempt to
destroy it (p. 143). When he left Walden Pond ... the evil
which lurked in institutions, he concluded, was more
malevolent than he had ever suspected as a youth. It was so
malevolent that it would have to be fought by every means
available, and that meant, of course, by attempting to
decrease the strength of institutions while at the same time

appealing to the conscience of man (pp. 133–34). The
method of reform from within, which he had advocated so
staunchly to 1845, had not been enough to arrest the trend,
any more than the combination of appeals to the conscience
and attacks on institutions to which he resorted after his stay
at Walden. The result was that by the end of the 1850's,
Thoreau was in a quandary, and willing to embrace any
method which seemed to have the least prospect of success
(p. 158). Though his close friends and admirers used the
[John Brown] incident in his defense [that through it he
fulfilled his social obligations], had they understood him they
would have gone to any length to play it down. For its real
meaning was that Thoreau's long cherished faith in the
adequacy of the Moral Law to satisfy all man's individual and
collective needs was slipping precariously (p. 215).

Since I have already discussed some of these points in an earlier chapter,
I will not amplify them here. But I am not convinced that Thoreau ever
more than wavered from his original principles. To the very end he held
to his belief that reform must come from within.

With government, as with reform, Thoreau's principles were
almost purely Transcendental. "There are, for Thoreau, only individuals
and the only fundamental law is the law of morality, and if political
expedience and the law of morality clash it becomes the duty of the
individual citizen to follow the divine law—that is, the voice of his
conscience within" (West, *Rebel Thought*, p. 206). He did not want "no
government, but *at once* a better government" (W, IV, 357), a
government that would "recognize the individual as a higher and
independent power, from which all its own power and authority are
derived" (W, IV, 387).

The government he idealized was not a government by force but
a government by co-operation. He fully realized that certain functions
could best be conducted by society rather than by the individual. "In
passage after passage of his published works and journal, Thoreau makes
specific proposals for legitimate governmental activity, often proposals
for new state or local laws or improvements of existing ones" (John C.
Broderick, "Thoreau's Proposals for Legislation," p. 285). "With
Thoreau the individual comes first, but the welfare of the community is

also important" (Broderick, "Thoreau's Principle of Simplicity," p. 286). Thoreau suggests compulsory education laws, supplemented by government-sponsored adult education. He asks that the government improve roads, issue adequate maps, further crime detection, prevent fires, and conserve natural resources. Thus, such a statement as that by James MacKaye (*Thoreau: The Philosopher of Freedom*, p. x), that Thoreau was "an extreme individualist, he never grasped the potentialities of cooperation in promoting efficient production," is belied. "It must be observed that almost all of Thoreau's proposals fall into a general grouping not unjustifiably described as welfare legislation" (Broderick, "Thoreau's Proposals for Legislation," p. 288). "The specific proposals in the journal, however, suggest Thoreau's acceptance of the principle of governmental activity, legislation for human welfare, so long as increased, abusive authority over the individual is not its inevitable companion" (p. 289).

Thoreau constantly kept in mind the danger of centralized government. No matter for what good purpose a government was established, it too soon became institutionalized. Founded to serve the individual, it inevitably ended in subordinating the individual to its own purposes. Founded to establish justice, it ended by preserving injustice. The protection of the institution of slavery by the federal, state, and even local governments of Thoreau's own time was to him convincing evidence of the inherent danger. It was the duty of the good citizen, he believed, to be ever on the watch to prevent the expansion of the powers of the state. Most, if not all, of his political essays were written to call the attention of his fellow citizens to this danger and to encourage them in their duty to fight it in specific instances.

At times, he found, one must be in outright revolt against the state. If the laws of the state came in conflict with the "higher laws" of the conscience, it was the conscience, not the state, that must be obeyed. It became a "duty of civil disobedience," and his essay on that subject has become, through the years, a manual of arms for those who are so led to revolt. It is significant that Thoreau, unlike his friends Hawthorne and Whitman, when he was faced with the dilemma of choosing between abolishing slavery and saving the Union, without hesitation chose the former.

Howard Floan complains that Thoreau's information about the true nature of slavery in the South was "both limited and distorted" (*The*

South in Northern Eyes, p. 63) because he had never visited the area and because he accepted prejudiced (that is, abolitionist) sources of information as accurate. But unlike most of his Northern contemporaries, Thoreau directed his attack not at the "far-off foes" in the South, "but at those in the North who were so enslaved by commerce that they were not capable of helping the Negro or the Mexican" (p. 66).

Far more important to Thoreau than government was liberty. That government he would respect that not only frees man from civil restraint but also fosters and encourages a true moral freedom:

> I please myself with imagining a State at last which can afford to be just to all men, and to treat the individual with respect as a neighbor; which even would not think it inconsistent with its own repose if a few were to live aloof from it, not meddling with it, nor embraced by it, who fulfilled all the duties of neighbors and fellow-men. A State which bore this kind of fruit, and suffered it to drop off as fast as it ripened, would prepare the way for a still more perfect and glorious State, which also I have imagined, but not yet anywhere seen (W, IV, 387).

Thoreau was even more critical of the prevailing economic system and for the same reason: means had become substituted for ends. It had become the major aim of business not to better mankind but to accumulate wealth for its own sake (W, II, 29). Thoreau thought the accumulation of surplus wealth was pointless. Not only that, it was dangerous. It "needlessly complicated existence and enslaved those who fell a prey to its allurements," Thoreau felt (William Kirchner, "Henry David Thoreau as a Social Critic," p. 42). The unfair distribution of wealth left many in dire need (J, III, 191), and ostentatious display of wealth was a direct incentive to crime (J, VII, 43).

Thoreau's measure of the value of money was "the amount of what I will call life which is required to be exchanged for it, immediately or in the long run" (W, II, 34). Thus he did not wish to purchase anything until he was convinced that it would produce for him ample reward for the labor required to pay for it. It was on this basis that he established his philosophy of the simple life.

The simple life, by whose gauge Henry Thoreau measured men and economies, aims at the most complete realization of the perfectibility innate in every person.... In his youth, Thoreau sought the conditions for such a life in an idealized distortion of the economic order then being displaced by the industrial revolution. After his experiment at Walden Pond, he moved toward a reconciliation between simplicity and an economy of machines and profit. This goal he never reached. But he left behind elements of a critique of our society and intimations of an undiminishable ideal to be fought for (Stoller, "Thoreau's Doctrine of Simplicity," p. 443).

Thoreau did not fear toil. Unlike most intellectuals, he was perfectly willing to perform manual labor if it were necessary to earn money to fulfill his needs. For a large portion of his adult life he earned his own living by surveying, manufacturing pencils, building chimneys, or even shoveling manure. But by reducing his wants, he found it was necessary to devote to such labor only a small portion of his time. Six weeks of labor produced funds sufficient to supply his wants for a year. As he said in his Harvard commencement essay, "The order of things should be somewhat reversed; the seventh should be man's day of toil, wherein to earn his living by the sweat of his brow; and the other six his Sabbath of the affections and the soul" (W, VI, 9). But even this one day of labor was to be chosen carefully. "The aim of the laborer should be, not to get his living, to get a 'good job,' but to perform well a certain work" (W, IV, 459). For "every man ... should love his work as much as the poet does his" (J, XIII, 20). "He advocated a leisure not in which to idle, but in which to seek self-improvement" (Kirchner, p. 117). The six days he spent, not in loafing but in pursuing his interests—observing nature and writing. The twenty volumes of his collected works are adequate proof of his industry.

For those who persisted in pursuing business and accumulating needless wealth, Thoreau had only contempt. "In my experience, nothing is so opposed to poetry [and to Thoreau poetry was the ideal]— not crime—as business" (J, IV, 162). Business led man astray, led him to ignore his higher nature, because it was not "simple, but artificial and complex" (J, V, 445). "If a man has spent all his days about some business, by which he has merely got to be rich, as it is called, *i.e.*, has got much money, many houses and barns and wood-lots, then his life has been a failure, I think" (J, XIV, 281).

Years ahead of his time, Thoreau saw the psychological dangers of division of labor. "However vital to industry division of labor might be, Thoreau was convinced that it thwarted that well-rounded self-culture he sought" (Kirchner, pp. 104–5). Visiting Sam Barrett's mill in Concord, Thoreau commented: "You come away from the great factory saddened, as if the chief end of man were to make pails; but, in the case of the countryman who makes a few by hand, rainy days, the relative importance of human life and of pails is preserved, and you come away, thinking of the simple and helpful life of the man" (J, XI, 227).

One of the most common stereotypes of Thoreau is that he was against civilization and wished to return to a primitive life. Like most such stereotypes, it is misleading. "Thoreau did not turn from the multiplicity of a modern world of mechanics, electricity, and radium, to look backward wistfully toward the age of faith in the Middle Ages, symbolized for Adams by the Virgin.... The setting of Walden is a geographical present" (Cook, *Passage to Walden*, p. 112). Over and over again Thoreau reiterated his love for the here and now: "We cannot afford not to live in the present" (W, V, 245). "Think of the consummate folly of attempting to get away from *here*! When the constant endeavor should be to get nearer and nearer *here*" (J, XI, 275).

Thoreau was satisfied to live in his own day and time, just as he would have been satisfied to live in any day or time he found himself in. But this did not prevent his being critical of the follies of his time. The Industrial Revolution was in full swing. Mechanization was the theme of the day. The railroad reached Concord just before Thoreau moved to Walden Pond, and before his death it had covered most of the eastern half of the United States. Mills were being established on every accessible water privilege in New England. New inventions were pouring into the patent office and on to the market. Paeans in praise of progress were being sung in every direction. Thoreau himself joined in the chorus when he could honestly admit the values of the accomplishments, but altogether too often, he saw, the new inventions were but "improved means to an unimproved end" (W, II, 58). Worse yet, we become so involved in the development of new improvements that we come to worship them for their own sake rather than for the better life they afford us. "Thoreau's originality was in accepting the advantages of civilization without sacrificing the benefits of the wild" (Broderick, "Thoreau's Principle of Simplicity," p. 279).

"There is no evidence that Thoreau ever held a brief for primitivism, beyond a recognition of its help in exposing the elementary necessaries for survival" (Christie, pp. 162–63). Indeed, quite in contrast with the popular concept of Thoreau as a primitivist is his own belief in progress. It is significant that so many of his works end on this note. Thus the closing words of *Walden*: "There is more day to dawn. The sun is but a morning star"; of "Life without Principle": "Why should we not ... congratulate each other on the ever-glorious morning?"; and of "Civil Disobedience": "Prepare the way for a still more perfect and glorious State." These surely are not the words of one who has lost faith in the progress of civilization.

Thoreau's lifetime was a period of urbanization. Large cities were a comparatively new phenomenon in America. But Thoreau was not pleased with their development. "Almost all our improvements, so called, tend to convert the country into the town," he complained (J, XIV, 57). He avoided cities whenever possible and said that the only places in Boston which appealed to him were the wharves, where he could look at the ocean, and the railroad station, where he could return to Concord. "He was convinced that cities, in their anxiety to exclude nature from within their limits and to impose the urban pattern upon the surrounding region, were destroying their own source of vitality" (Broderick, "Thoreau's Principle of Simplicity," p. 107). He noted that "artificial, denaturalized persons cannot handle nature without being poisoned. If city-bred girls visit their country cousins,—go a-berrying with them,—they are sure to return covered with blueberry bumps at least" (J, VIII, 448–49). Cities, by separating man from nature, worked an irreparable harm. "At the same time that we exclude mankind from gathering berries in our field, we exclude them from gathering health and happiness.... We strike only one more blow at a simple and wholesome relation to nature" (J, XIV, 56). There is a constant need for the urbanized man to return to nature to fulfill his spiritual needs. The symbol of Romulus and Remus, the founders of Rome, being raised by a wolf, was a favorite in Thoreau's mythology.

However, it should be noted, as Broderick has pointed out, in his later years Thoreau came to accept the value of cities as repositories of human knowledge in their libraries and museums.

In *Walden* particularly Thoreau made much of his desire for solitude. But one must be careful not to think him antisocial. When he traveled through the Maine woods and discovered true hermits living miles from any neighbor, he was appalled. He wanted merely to be able to be alone when he felt the need to be by himself, not to dwell in complete solitude.

Actually, Thoreau was a man of many friendships. First and foremost were the members of his own family. The closeness of his ties with them is emphasized in his letters. Both his sisters and his parents always spoke of him as a most devoted brother and son.

Second, he had a large number of intellectual companions, particularly among the Transcendentalists. His friendship with Emerson is well known. He was on even closer terms of intimacy with Ellery Channing, who accompanied him on his daily walks. There is no need of listing here the many others he turned to for intellectual stimulation.

Third, there were the children. Edward Emerson, in his *Henry Thoreau as Remembered by a Young Friend*, has left adequate evidence of the esteem in which he was held by the small folk of Concord. Thoreau's later *Journals* are filled with notations of visits from children, telling him of their discoveries of wild flowers or birds. When he died, the local schools were closed so the children might follow his cortege and place wild flowers on his grave.

And, finally, there were the townspeople of Concord. Thoreau here exerted his individuality in his choice of friends. In his *Journal* we find comparatively little mention of the leading citizens. They did not interest him. He had little more interest in the typical farmers of his neighborhood. Their lives were too mean; like the businessmen, they were too concerned with making money (J, XII, 366). "The farmer accustomed to look at his crops from a mercenary point of view is not aware how beautiful they are" (J, XIII, 414). He was more concerned with the "poetical farmers"—Hosmer, Minott, and Rice (J, III, 41)—because they seemed to be living closer to the life he idealized. And perhaps even more he was attracted to the social outcasts—Melvin, Goodwin, and Alek Therien, the French-Canadian wood chopper. These men had the courage to live the life they wanted, and for that he admired them, even though some of them drank to excess and lived outside the bounds of Victorian standards.

Included with the social outcasts were the Irish. The modern liberal is occasionally offended by Thoreau's critical comments on the

Irish immigrants who flocked into New England in the 1840's. He criticized their uncleanliness, their shiftlessness, and their lack of veracity. He thus reflected the strong prejudice of the old Yankee stock, a prejudice based in large part on the fact that the Irish were Roman Catholics. But as time went by and he became better acquainted, his attitude changed and he learned to admire their industry. He helped the illiterate to write back to the old country, defended one laborer when he was unjustly deprived by his Yankee employer of a prize he had won at the local cattle show, and collected subscriptions to enable another Irishman to bring his family across the Atlantic. "Although Thoreau's portrayal of the Irish is less important than his experiences with nature or his lessons in economic values, it has a significance that cannot be overlooked. In its freedom from religious and political bias it is almost unique as a contemporary record" (Buckley, p. 400).

Thoreau's whole life was a search. "His life was a quest of the Holy Grail, undertaken in all purity of body and mind and soul, and in the fullness of faith and devotion" (Norman Foerster, "The Humanism of Thoreau," p. 9). As Thoreau himself says in *Walden*: "I wished to live deliberately, to front only the essential facts of life, and see if I could not learn what it had to teach, and not, when I came to die, discover that I had not lived" (W, II, 100–101).

Although he would have been the first to admit (as he does in his parable of the hound, bay horse, and turtledove in *Walden*) that the perfect life was an unattainable ideal, he was convinced at an early age of the direction in which to aim. It was "the perfect correspondence of Nature to man, so that he is at home with her" (J, X, 127). "I love to see anything that implies a simpler mode of life and a greater nearness to the earth" (J, XIV, 88). "In society you will not find health, but in nature. You must converse much with the field and woods, if you would imbibe such health into your mind and spirit as you covet for your body.... Without that our feet at least stood in the midst of nature, all our faces would be pale and livid" (J, I, 306). It was for this that he wished to live a life of leisure—so that he might spend as much time as possible with nature.

Thoreau frequently said: "I think that I cannot preserve my health and spirits, unless I spend four hours a day at least—and it is commonly more than that—sauntering through the woods and over the hills and fields, absolutely free from all worldly engagements" (W, V, 207). It was for this reason he disliked cities. They denied man his opportunity of communing with nature. It was for this also that he condemned the businessmen and upstanding citizens of his community. They were too busy to commune with nature. The world was too much with them, or rather, they were too much with the world.

He saw a close association with nature as a means toward a fuller life. It was a purgative, a panacea for the ills of civilization: "I have come to this hill to see the sun go down, to recover sanity and put myself again in relation with Nature" (J, VI, 329). "Nature, the earth herself, is the only panacea. They bury poisoned sheep up to the necks in earth to take the poison out of them" (J, XII, 350). "It is important, then, that we should air our lives from time to time by removals, and excursions into the fields and woods,—starve our vices" (J, XII, 343).

It was an almost inevitable corollary of Thoreau's search for the ideal life that he should become involved in a search for the ideal man; that is, the man in perfect correspondence with nature: "It is the marriage of the soul with Nature that makes the intellect fruitful, that gives birth to imagination" (J, II, 413).

Wherever Thoreau traveled in history he was in search of men who had fulfilled his vision of manhood, who lived close to nature and understood it (Lawrence Willson, "The Influence of Early North American History and Legend," p. 181). His concern to know just how far men *had* taken advantage of their opportunities perhaps explains better than anything else ... the reason for his historical research (p. 149). In the last analysis, all of Thoreau's excursions into antiquarianism and history were inspired by the same motive that inspired his excursions into the woods and up and down the rivers; to learn more about the basic relationship in which man and nature stood to each other (p. 86). When he considered the Concord Fight, it was to discover the manhood displayed in it; when he read the "Wast Books" of Ephraim Jones, it was to discover the independence of general stores and the merchandise of the eighteenth century villager (p. 83).

He investigated the history of the Pilgrims and the Jesuit missionaries and the *coureurs de bois* [because] in their lives he thought he would be able to see more clearly than in the lives of his contemporaries the workings of divine law, because they had perforce lived closer to nature, where the permanency of that law and its inexorableness were most openly demonstrable. But in each of these studies he failed in some degree to discover what he wished to discover. The men of old Concord were brave, to be sure, but their bravery was expended merely in an effort to reduce the tax on their tea. The Pilgrims were spiritual pioneers with a grand and thrilling motive, but they had strayed away from the motive to follow the hire of the commercial spirit. They had lived on nature rather than in it. The *coureurs de bois* had been mere adventurers, looking for lives of titillated ease. The heroic Jesuits had been held in thrall by a small and foolish superstition. In each enterprise the idealism had somehow failed (pp. 222–23).

Disillusioned with the pioneer Americans, Thoreau turned to the Indian in his search. In his *Journal* for 1841 he wrote, "The charm of the Indian to me is that he stands free and unconstrained in Nature, is her inhabitant and not her guest, and wears her easily and gracefully" (J , I, 253). Thoreau felt "the Indian could teach the white man, who was pathetically involved in his self-created civilization, the necessity of a more congenial *rapport* with a natural environment" (Cook, *Passage to Walden*, p. 87). But eventually, as he grew older, he became disillusioned and disappointed because "the Indian had made no attempt to cultivate the spiritual side of his being" (Willson, "The Influence of Early North American History and Legend," p. 280). "In the case of the savage," Thoreau says in his *Journal* (V, 410), "the accompaniment of simplicity is idleness with its attendant vices, but in the case of the philosopher, it is the highest employment and development."

Thoreau was led to admire the hunters and trappers of Concord, men such as Haines, Melvin, and Goodwin, who, because of their closeness to nature, were outcasts in the eyes of most Concordians. Twice he speaks of Haines's reminding him of the Indian (J , VI, 233; J, III, 290). And again he says: "The woodcutter and his practices and experiences are more to be attended to; his accidents, perhaps more than any other's, should mark the epochs in the winter day. Now that the Indian is gone, he stands nearest to nature" (J , III, 244). But again, as did the Indian, they had one serious failing: they lacked a spiritual, an aesthetic sense. Nowhere in the past or in the present could Thoreau find his ideal mail. He could only hope that such a man would develop in the future. He concentrated therefore upon developing such a man. And consistent with his philosophy, he began with himself.

The search for beauty was one of the primary motivations in Thoreau's life. It is impossible to read at any length in any of his writings without becoming aware of that fact. Beauty, along with goodness and truth, was one of the members of the trinity he substituted for the orthodox Christian Trinity. It is surprising, therefore, to discover that he devotes little space to exposition of an aesthetic theory. Charles Reid Metzger, after attempting to study Thoreau's aesthetics, comes to the conclusion that "what Thoreau had to say about art in general ... is too fragmentary and too vague to be dignified by the title art theory" ("The Transcendental Esthetics in America," p. 237). "Thoreau sought to experience beauty rather than apprehend principles" (p. 252). Virtually the only time he made any extended attempt to formulate an aesthetic theory occurred in the spring of 1852 after a reading of the works of William Gilpin on the picturesque. But even then his interest centered primarily on natural beauty rather than formal art. "He had the artist's eye for whatever beauty he found in nature, but of art as such he had almost no knowledge or appreciation" (Huffert, "Thoreau as a Teacher," p. 408). "What is a gallery in the house to a gallery in the streets!" Thoreau wrote. "I think that there is not a picture-gallery in the country which would be worth so much to us as is the western view under the elms of our main street" (J, XI, 220).

We can search in vain through Thoreau's writings for any extended comments on any of the great masterpieces of painting or sculpture. They were simply outside his ken. For Thoreau "the highest condition of art is artlessness" (J, I, 153) and he found more beauty in an ink blot than in a formal painting (J, I, 119). "The too exquisitely cultured" he avoided as he did the theater (J, IV, 154).

The plastic arts appealed to him a little more, and he was impressed when he discovered an Indian stone pestle fashioned into the likeness of a bird. It convinced him that the Indian had "so far begun to leave behind him war, and even hunting, and to redeem himself from the savage state" (J, V, 526). But even sculpture, to meet his approval, had to be representative rather than abstract, and the more it was akin to nature, the greater its appeal for him (J, I, 380).

Thoreau had a lifelong interest in music. But he was more interested in the music of nature than in the music of man: "One will lose no music by not attending oratorios and operas" (J, II, 379). "I get my new experiences still, not at the opera listening to the Swedish Nightingale [Jenny Lind], but at Beck Stow's Swamp listening to the native wood thrush" (J, IX, 43).

It was for architecture that Thoreau reserved his greatest interest, and his aesthetic approach was primarily functional. In this he anticipated such modern creative geniuses as Frank Lloyd Wright and Louis Sullivan. Wright wrote me (February 28, 1952), "The history of American Architecture would be incomplete without Thoreau's wise observations on the subject."

Thoreau says in *Walden* (p. 52):

> What of architectural beauty I now see, I know has gradually grown from within outward, out of the necessities and character of the indweller, who is the only builder.... The most interesting dwellings in this country, as the painter knows, are the most unpretending, humble log huts and cottages of the poor commonly; it is the life of the inhabitants whose shells they are, and not any peculiarity in their surfaces merely, which makes them *Picturesque*.

As he strove for simplicity and economy in his life, he strove for simplicity and economy in his art. He was not alone in this, for Emerson, Horatio Greenough, and Walt Whitman, approaching the problem from different angles, each arrived at the same concept at approximately the same time. But Thoreau was perhaps the most practical and the most concrete of the four. Yet I do not wish to imply that Thoreau's approach to architecture was purely from the standpoint of economy. He was able to appreciate the beauty of the functional approach. The functional building, he thought, blended into its background. He even suggested that "the architect take a hint from the pyramidal or conical form of the muskrat's house.... Something of this form and color, like a large haycock in the meadow, would be in harmony with the scenery" (J, IV, 423). The early American houses were "earth-loving"; they needed "no coping of bricks to catch the eye, no alto or basso relievo" (J, III, 34). In contrast, the Victorian house of Thoreau's own period, with its gingerbread ornamentation and sugar-coating, was offensive to his eye.

Thoreau's interest in the field of education has been generally ignored; yet it was a subject that concerned him most of his life. The principles he put into practice in his own school were a distinct foreshadowing of modern progressive education. "Nature study, local history, physical education, and nature appreciation were integrated to an extent not yet achieved on a wide scale in our own day" (Huffert, p. 413). A good part of the school day was spent out of doors, in hiking, rowing, swimming, and observing natural history and local history in the field. Thoreau advocated the introduction of nature studies into the elementary schools fifty years before it was in general use (pp. 376–77). "Learning by doing" is John Dewey's phrase, but Thoreau put the concept into practice years before Dewey.

In disciplinary methods Thoreau was equally progressive. He resigned his position in the Concord public schools rather than use physical force. To Orestes Brownson he wrote (December 30, 1837), "I have ever been disposed to regard the cowhide as a non-conductor." And when he established his own school, he used understanding and an appeal to the moral sense of the child as his principal disciplinary devices.

The basis for his whole educational theory was that the child was innately good and that it was the purpose of the school to foster and stimulate the child's inner development toward perfection. As I have pointed out earlier, Thoreau was convinced that paradise could be achieved on this earth through the full development of man's potentialities, and all his educational philosophy was aimed in that direction.

Thoreau was consistently critical of the collegiate education of his day. He once remarked to Emerson that Harvard taught all the branches of learning but got to none of the roots. Too much time was spent in studying theory, too little in actual practice: "To my astonishment I was informed on leaving college that I had studied navigation!" he says in *Walden* (p. 57); "—why, if I had taken one turn down the harbor I should have known more about it." He rejoiced when, some years after his graduation, Harvard established a school of science (W, VI, 118). But on the other hand, he did not deny the value of a liberal education: "The learning of trades and professions which is designed to enable men to earn their living, or to fit them for a particular station in life—is *servile*" (J, XIII, 15).

He was critical of college faculties. There were "professors of philosophy, but not philosophers" (W, II, 16). They were not interested in searching for truth, but lived in the shadow of their established institutions and spent their time defending the *status quo*. True educators, he believed, should broaden their students' horizons; they should at least teach the students "where the arsenal is, in case they should ever want to use any of its weapons" (J, XIII, 67). All the while he was at Harvard, he wrote his class secretary later, "My spirit yearned for the sympathy of my old and almost forgotten friend Nature."

A further contribution by Thoreau was his interest in adult education, expressed primarily through the lyceum movement of his day. He was an active member of the Concord Lyceum from its founding in 1829 until his death, lecturing before it nineteen times and serving several terms as its curator. In the mid-forties he was one of the leaders of the successful movement to permit controversial subjects such as abolitionism to be discussed from the lyceum platform. And in *Walden* he urged his fellow townsmen to devote more funds to the lyceum even at the expense of omitting one bridge over a river (pp. 121–22).

From an early point in his career, probably as early as 1840, Thoreau considered himself a professional writer, and throughout his career he was vitally interested in the craft of writing. One could make a fairly sizable collection of his comments on the subject. Yet, "it is doubtful that Thoreau was systematic or purposeful enough or even original enough to warrant being considered among the first rank of American critical writers" (George Craig, "Literary Criticism in the Works of Henry David Thoreau," p. 5). "Thoreau's interest in technique was normally limited to a concern with his own technique. When he discusses other writers, his concern is more with emotional impact" (p. 141).

It is surprising that "within the twenty-six printed volumes by Thoreau and beyond them in unpublished manuscripts there are several hundred pages of literary criticism, yet one finds few pages, perhaps a total of ten, in which Thoreau concerns himself with discussing the duties of a critic and the function of criticism" (Adams, "Henry Thoreau's Literary Theory and Criticism," p. 120). Thoreau said so little on the subject, Adams feels, because Wordsworth, Coleridge, Carlyle, and the other early romanticists had already so well formulated his ideas that he felt no need of re-expressing them.

> Though there is not one new element in Thoreau's critical theory, there is not another theory like it in all particulars or even in outline. Thoreau laid emphases where they had not been laid before. He worked out some of his critical dicta to

lengths that had not been attempted hitherto. He was always running some theory down to its ultimate end.

For instance no other transcendentalist stated the "labor doctrine" so forcefully or persistently, though virtually all transcendentalists held it.... No one else spoke so affectionately, so personally of Nature as the ally of the poet, though a hundred critics before Thoreau's time had considered nature as a source of inspiration.... Health may long have been the subject of those who sought in some measure to account for genius, but few critics have so consistently demanded health as a basis for true poetry (pp. 166–67).

The recent growth of interest in the organic theory of literature has quite naturally focused attention on Thoreau as one of its outstanding proponents. Fred W. Lorch, in "Thoreau and the Organic Principle in Poetry," has made the most authoritative study of the subject, and in summary says:

In conceiving of poetry as something that grows like an organism in nature rather than as something that is "made," Thoreau reveals his discipleship to the organic theorists. He believed the source of the poet's intuition to be the divine and universal Intelligence, which expresses itself and comes to poetic fruition through the agency of the poet; and that genius, or the divine element in the poet, and talent, the human element, are both essential in poetic expression. Thoreau failed to differentiate clearly between the conception on the one hand that outer form is the imitation of inner form, and the conception on the other that form is organic, but despite this confusion, he customarily regarded form as an inherent quality of the intuition, which proceeds from within outward. Beauty is both *essentially* and *ethically* organic. Poetry is the fruit of the poet; it grows like an organism from the soul of the poet's character; and consequently, the nobility of a poem is a symbol of the nobility of the poet. The highest function of poetry is the improvement of man. The purest poetry manifests itself not primarily in a poem "written and done," but in the character of the poet; the finest poem is the life-poem. Thoreau's conception of the organic principle [thus] ... suggests an approach to a better understanding of his efforts at self-improvement (pp. 48–49).

It is surprising that although Thoreau was always vitally concerned with form, he has been continually criticized for the formlessness of his works. "Thoreau's books are formless.... His emphasis was much on *matter* and very little on *manner*," says Raymond Adams (p. 102). "In 'Walden' the sentences bear no more plastic relation to each other than do the stones of the cairn which now marks the site of Thoreau's hut," adds J. B. Atkinson in "Concerning Thoreau's Style." Perhaps it was Thoreau's own description of his method of composition that led them to these conclusions: "From all points of the compass, from the earth beneath and the heavens above, have come these inspirations and been entered duly in the order of their arrival in the journal. Thereafter, when the time arrived, they were winnowed into lectures, and again, in due time, from lectures into essays" (J, I, 413). "When I select one here and another there, and strive to join sundered thoughts, I make but a partial heap after all," he complains at another point (J, I, 199–200). But they reckoned without the extensive revision and amalgamation to which Thoreau subjected all his work. "Seldom have I known an author who made more drafts of what he might sometime print, or more persistently revised what he had once composed," wrote F. B. Sanborn (*The Life of Henry David Thoreau*, p. 55), who handled so many of his manuscripts. "I wish that I could buy at the shops some kind of india-rubber that would rub out at once all that in my writing which it now costs me so many perusals, so many months if not years, and so much reluctance, to erase," Thoreau complained (J, VI, 30). Recent research (see Shanley's study of *Walden* and Hovde's of *A Week*, in Chapter Two, for example) has confirmed the tremendous amount of revision to which Thoreau subjected his work. It has also demonstrated that the labor was worth while. It is the unanimous opinion of those critics who have examined his manuscripts in their various stages that Thoreau revised and reworked his papers with great skill.

Early critics tended to think of Thoreau as a master of the sentence. Lowell in 1865 said, "There are sentences of his as perfect as anything in the language." By 1906 Bradford Torrey saw that "the sentences might be complete in themselves, detachable, able to stand alone, but the paragraph never lacked a logical and even formal cohesion" (*Friends on the Shelf*, p. 126). In recent years critics have at last begun to realize the essential unity of his books as wholes. Most obvious was Thoreau's use of the unity of time. In *A Week* he used the seven days of the week for chapter divisions (although his journey had actually taken two weeks); in *Cape Cod* he unified three separate excursions into one narrative; and in *Walden* he adopted the device most successfully, combining the adventures of two years and two months into one year, and using the circle of the seasons to trace symbolically his spiritual growth. Indeed, *Walden* is a masterwork of integrated form, and Sherman Paul's brilliant discussion of its structure (see Chapter Two, above) should silence any further charges that Thoreau lacked the ability to unify his work.

"It is not in man to determine what his style shall be. He might as well determine what his thoughts shall be." Thus wrote Thoreau in his essay on Carlyle (W, IV, 330). But whether it was consciously or unconsciously created, Thoreau's style has long won admiration. "His literary style has not been excelled by any other essayist in our literature," says Adaline Conway in *The Essay in American Literature* (p. 68).

Perhaps the most notable characteristic of Thoreau's style is the concreteness of his diction. Abstractness, abstruseness, and often vapidness were altogether too frequently characteristics of his fellow Transcendentalists' styles—even that of Emerson. But these are charges that can rarely, if ever, be brought against Thoreau except in his early apprenticeship.

He loved homely, down-to-earth phrases such as "finger-cold," "a jag of wood," "apple-pie order," and "full of the devil." He loved "good old English words" (J, III, 41), words "that can be traced back to a Celtic original" (J, III, 232–33). Indeed, he was prone to go off on an etymological digression at the least provocation—or with none at all. He was delighted when his rural neighbors, especially George Minott, "the most poetical farmer in Concord," sent him to his dictionary with an Elizabethan word usage. It is not surprising therefore to discover that he had twenty-nine dictionaries and grammars in his library. On the other hand, although his vocabulary was large (note his use of such words as

"sempiternal," "fuscous," "susurrus," "crepusculum," and "sesquipedalian"),
he was not pedantic. He complained: "A writer who does not speak out
of a full experience uses torpid words, wooden or lifeless words, such
words as 'humanitary,' which have a paralysis in their tails" (J, IV, 225;
see also J, X, 261). And he also complained: "When I read some of the
rules for speaking and writing the English language correctly,—as that a
sentence must never end with a particle,—and perceive how implicitly
even the learned obey it, I think—

> Any fool can make a rule
> And every fool will mind it. " (J, XIII, 125)

He thought that "the first requisite and rule [of grammar] is that
expression shall be vital and natural" (J, XI, 386).

One of the few affectations in his use of words was his occasional
tendency (although not nearly so pronounced as Emerson's) to use
archaic words and forms, such as "fain," "methinks," "wot," "clomb,"
and "blowed." Another was his affinity for Indian words; he referred to
the muskrat as the "musquash," and wished that Lakeville,
Massachusetts, had been named "Assawampsett" or "Sanacus" (J, VIII,
395).

His style is highly figurative, filled with similes, metaphors,
hyperbole, and synecdoche. I once checked a list of more than fifty
different types of figures of speech against *Walden* and found virtually
every one represented, most of them many times over. As one might
expect, a large percentage of the figures are based on nature. "Natural
objects and phenomena are the original symbols or types which express
our thoughts and feelings," he believed (J, V, 135; see also J, XII, 389).
"River and lake images are the most fundamental in Thoreau, and have
implications not yet fully read. The river 'of our thoughts' is the
dominant figure for the *Week*" (William Drake, "A Formal Study of
Thoreau," p. 18). Although John Broderick and Sherman Paul (see
Chapter Two) have made a good start at examining more closely the
images of Thoreau's writing, much more work needs to be done.

The chief error of many of Thoreau's critics, from Lowell on
down, is that they fail to detect his humor. They accept him literally
despite his many warnings that he was an exaggerator who liked to "brag
as lustily as chanticleer" (W, II, 94).

Harold Guthrie asserts that "a proper adjustment of our critical view of Thoreau's humor is not only important in itself, but ... it is also essential to a just and complete view of the man and his works" ("The Humor of Thoreau," p. 1). "The dangers and demerits of a paradoxical style are sufficiently obvious; and no writer has ever been less careful than Thoreau to safeguard himself against misunderstandings on this score. He has consequently been much misunderstood, and will always be so, save where the reader brings to his task a certain amount of sympathy and kindred sense of humor" (Salt, *The Life of Henry D. Thoreau*, p. 263).

That Thoreau had a well-developed sense of humor is obvious on examination of both his writings and the memoirs of his friends such as Sanborn, Charming, and Edward Emerson. Indeed, be expounds his principles of humor quite explicitly in his essay on Thomas Carlyle. "His humor is an inseparable part of the man and his writings; ... it is based on good nature and love of fun, and ... his sole negative qualification for humor in general is that it should never be merely idle nor frankly degrading" (Guthrie, p. 51). "Thoreau's humor could be warmly human" (p. 48). And "a list of the things he considered laughable ... reveals a normal, unsophisticated New Englander,—sane, genial, even fun-loving" (p. 47). Thus Lowell, in saying that Thoreau was without humor, clearly missed the point of most of his writing. And when Stevenson condemned Thoreau as a prig for expurgating humorous passages from his writings, he did not realize that Thoreau was merely trying to "reduce the egotistical, deliberately humorous passages" (p. 39).

"Thoreau believed that a general function, or service of humor, especially in all forms of 'transcendental' writings, is to provide a leaven that renders it digestible" (p. 90). One of Thoreau's aims was humorously to satirize the follies and vices of men (p. 92). "His moral censure and satirical disquisitions ... are but the reverse side of his life-long search for truth" (p. 93).

"If Thoreau continually employs humor in his writings, and if that humor is often paradoxical, exaggerative, and metaphorical, then a literal reading of his works which takes no account of his humor, must inevitably result in frequent misapprehension of his meaning" (p. 106). Indeed, George Ripley, James Russell Lowell, Emerson, Alcott, Ellery Charming, and Stevenson all misinterpreted Thoreau because they thus misread his humor. Salt was the first to understand the true function of humor in Thoreau's writings.

Guthrie thus analyzes Thoreau's humor:

> Thoreau generally laughs at, not the unconventional or bizarre in human behaviour, but the conventional.... Unthinking conformity to foolish tradition rouses Thoreau's sharpest laughter, and since some of his readers are incapable of sharing his point of view, they are more irritated than amused by his humor (p. 17).

> [Thoreau] disavowed the practice of humor as an end in itself (p.109). His real calling is to expose and discountenance all forms of human folly and vice, for it is Thoreau's conviction that "if we only see clearly enough how mean our lives are, they will be splendid enough." His favorite weapon for the extirpation of such meanness is a genial humor of exaggeration, paradox, and metaphor; but occasionally, when the meanness appears to him outrageous, his moral indignation finds vent in bitter irony and sardonic word-play which are, closer to invective than raillery (p. 109). His goal is to free as many minds as possible by humorously exposing the meanness and desperation of conventional modes of thought and behaviour (p. 115a).

> Certainly a reading of [Walden] which mistakes Thoreau's humorous overstatement and genial satire for splenetic and uncompromising assertion must result in the impression that Thoreau counseled his readers to renounce society completely (p. 117). [But] Thoreau's true position, clearly, is not a renunciation of society but a carefully qualified acceptance of such social institutions and practices as do not degrade men nor dissipate their energies (pp. 122–23). Thoreau's social and economic views, when examined in the light of humorous satire, appear actually quite moderate (p. 129). For those who understand it, his satirical attacks on men and institutions arouse, not resentment and counterattack, but laughter and a return to our senses (p. 151).

As Raymond Adams has pointed out, the mock-heroic is one of Thoreau's standard humorous devices. Not only does he use it in such well-known passages as the battle of the ants in *Walden*, but it is also the basic pattern of the whole of *A Week*. Use of this technique permitted him to approach in prose the close-up photography of present-day naturalists. Later nature writers seized upon his use of the mock-heroic and incorporated it into their writings so that he brought about "a literature of nature such as had not existed before" ("Thoreau's Mock-Heroics and the American Natural History Writers," p. 97).

It is surprising that Thoreau's abilities for characterization have not been more widely recognized. Note, for example, his "Dutch sailor with a singular bullfrog or trilobite expression of the eyes, whose eyes were like frog ponds in the broad platter of his cheeks and gleamed like a pool covered with frog-spittle" (J, II, 79). Or Mrs. Field, "with the never absent mop in one hand, and yet no effects of it visible anywhere" (W, II, 227). Or the "regular countrywoman with half an acre of face" (J, VII, 476). A novelist friend of mine once told me after noting several such descriptions that she mourned the fact that Thoreau never tried his hand at writing fiction.

But fiction to Thoreau was for entertainment. And he was writing not to entertain but to enlighten. He deliberately avoided the striking, the sensational.

> I omit the unusual—the hurricanes and earthquakes—and describe the common.... You may have the extraordinary for your province, if you will let me have the ordinary. Give me the obscure life, the cottage of the poor and humble, the workdays of the world, the barren fields, the smallest share of all things but poetic perception (J, II, 428–29). I know that no subject is too trivial for me.... The theme is nothing, the life is everything. All that interests the reader is the depth and intensity of the life excited.... Give me simple, cheap, and homely themes (J, IX, 121).

That Thoreau had that "poetic perception" goes almost without saying. "Great art consists in the imaginative heightening of the immediate," says R. W. B. Lewis. And therein lies Thoreau's greatest strength. He makes us see all that which lies around us, but which, until he pointed it out, we never saw before.

One final word must be spoken on Thoreau's ideas. Thoreau was a critic of society, but primarily a positive rather than a negative critic. "There are many statements in the writings of Thoreau, which taken together, seem to indicate that he was a thorough-going pessimist and a hater of mankind.... But these statements ... are merely the ... statements of the ... idealist who loved men too well to see them tossing aside their opportunities for moral and intellectual growth and the good life" (Lawrence Willson, "The Influence of Early North American History and Legend," p. 153). "It was not his carelessness of man's good but the precise opposite, his passion for it, that made him denounce so bitterly the society into which he was born and to assume the part of the gadfly stinging it into virtue" (Norman Foerster, *Nature in American Literature*, p. 137). "Probably he himself would have been distressed to think that he might be remembered chiefly as a satirist or a critic; as a man who had managed to convey only his dissatisfaction with the world and not the happiness which he believed to have been his" (Krutch, p. 276).

Basically Thoreau's life was a happy one. A few weeks before he died he wrote a letter to Myron Benton (March 21, 1862) saying, "I have not many months to live.... I may add that I am enjoying existence as much as ever, and regret nothing." Of all the many and varied titles Thoreau has been given, perhaps none is more felicitous than Hildegarde Hawthorne's "Concord's Happy Rebel."

SOURCES

The two most detailed studies of Thoreau's ideas are Joseph Wood Krutch, *Henry David Thoreau* (New York, 1948) and Reginald L. Cook, *Passage to Walden* (Boston, 1949). Henry Seidel Canby, "Henry David Thoreau," in *Classic Americans* (New York, 1931, pp. 184–225), is a thoughtful brief analysis. Louis B. Salomon, "The Practical Thoreau" (*CE*, XVII, 1956, 229–32), refutes eight of the commonest misinterpretations of Thoreau's ideas with specific quotations from his writings. However, in reply see Wade Thompson, "The Impractical Thoreau" (*CE*, XIX, 1957, 67–70). One of the few studies to deal with the gradual development and change of Thoreau's ideas is William Drake, "A Formal Study of Thoreau" (Iowa University, M.A., 1948). It would be a great service to Thoreau scholars to have this work in print and to have its implications studied further.

Mary Edith Cochnower, "Thoreau and Stoicism" (Iowa University, Ph.D., 1938), is the only detailed study of the stoic element in Thoreau's life and philosophy.

An early but still provocative study of the Transcendentalist basis of Thoreau's thought is Daniel Gregory Mason, "The Idealistic Basis of Thoreau's Genius" (*Harvard Monthly*, XXV, 1897, 82–93). For an analysis of Thoreau's use of sound as the agency of Transcendental correspondence in achieving the mystical experience, see Sherman Paul, "The Wise Silence" (*NEQ*, XXII, 1949, 511–27).

For Thoreau's influence on the development of the natural history essay, see Philip Marshall Hicks, *The Development of the Natural History Essay in American Literature* (Philadelphia, 1924); Richard E. Haymaker, "The Out-of-Door Essay" in his *From Pampas to Hedgerows and Downs: A Study of W. H. Hudson* (New York, 1954, pp. 45–84); and Reginald Cook, "Nature's Eye-Witness" in his *Passage to Walden*. See also Henry Chester Tracy, *American Naturists* (New York, 1930), Alec Lucas, "Thoreau, Field Naturalist" (*UTQ*; XXIII, 1954, 227–32), and Robert Henry Welker, "Literary Birdman: Henry David Thoreau" in *Birds & Men* (Cambridge, Mass., 1955, pp. 91–115), which traces Thoreau's changing attitude toward ornithology. See also Hans Huth, *Nature and the American* (Berkeley, Calif., 1957).

For disparaging comments on Thoreau's ability as a naturalist, see Francis Allen, *Thoreau's Bird-Lore* (Boston, 1925), Fannie Hardy Eckstorm, "Thoreau's 'Maine Woods'" (*Atlantic Monthly*, CII, 1908, 242–50; *TCC*); W. L. McAtee, "Adaptationist Naïveté" (*Scientific Monthly*, XLVIII, 1939, 253–55); and John Burroughs, "Another Word on Thoreau" in *The Last Harvest* (Boston, 1922, pp. 103–71).

For Thoreau's work with Agassiz, see *Familiar Letters* (W, VI, 125–32); with Harris, see Joseph Wade, "Friendship of Two Old-Time Naturalists" (*Scientific Monthly*, XXIII, 1926, 152–60). Edward S. Deevey's study of Thoreau's limnology will be found in "A Re-examination of Thoreau's 'Walden'" (*Quarterly Review of Biology*, XVII, 1942, 1–11). Leo Stoller, "A Note on Thoreau's Place in the History of Phenology" (*Isis*, XLVII, 1956, 172–81), cites Leopold's comment and refutes it. Thoreau's importance to the nature study movement is evaluated in Anna Botsford Comstock, "Henry David Thoreau" (*Nature and Science Education Review*, II, 1930, 49–55).

For further studies of Thoreau's science, see Raymond Adams, "Thoreau's Science" (*Scientific Monthly*, LX, 1945, 379–82), perhaps the best discussion to date of Thoreau's gradually changing attitude toward science; Lee Marten Nash, "Ecology in the Writings of Henry David Thoreau" (University of Washington, M.A., 1951); Ludlow Griscom, *Birds of Concord* (Cambridge, Mass., 1949); Joseph Wade, "Some Insects of Thoreau's Writings" (*Journal of the New York Entomological Society*, XXXV, 1927, 1–21), a thorough summary and evaluation of his comments on insects; Kathryn Whitford, "Thoreau and the Woodlots of Concord" (*NEQ*, XXIII, 1950, 291–306), the best evaluation of Thoreau's findings in his "Succession of Forest Trees"; Philip and Kathryn Whitford, "Thoreau: Pioneer Ecologist and Conservationist" (*Scientific Monthly*, LXXIII, 1951, 291–96; *TCC*); H. S. Canby, "What He Lived For" in *Thoreau* (Boston, 1939, pp. 322–42); Charles Reid Metzger, "The Transcendental Esthetics in America" (University of Washington, Ph.D., 1954, pp. 202–12), which discusses Thoreau as a taxonomist and ecologist; and Reginald Cook, *Passage to Walden* (Boston, 1949, pp. 173–204), which discusses Thoreau's attitude toward science and nature, as does William H. Kirchner, "Henry David Thoreau as a Social Critic" (University of Minnesota, Ph.D., 1938, pp. 155–77). Reginald Heber Howe, "Thoreau, the Lichenist" (*Guide to Nature*, May, 1912, 17–20), anthologizes Thoreau's comments on lichens. See also Charles Metzger, "Thoreau on Science" (*Annals of Science*, XII, 1956, 206–11).

The major discussion of Thoreau's theology is John Sylvester Smith, "The Philosophical Naturism of Henry David Thoreau" (Drew University, Ph.D., 1948). Briefer studies include Harry Elmore Hurd, "The Religion of Henry David Thoreau" (*Christian Leader*, August 25 and September 1, 1928), and R. Lester Mondale, "Henry David Thoreau and the Naturalizing of Religion" (*Unity*, CXXXVII, 1951, 14–17). Reginald Cook discusses Thoreau's mysticism in *Passage to Walden* (pp. 122–43). Raymond Adams summarizes Thoreau's attitude toward an afterlife in "Thoreau and Immortality" (*SP*, XXVI, 1929, 58–66), using a number of unpublished Thoreau manuscripts. I have written a brief note on Thoreau's reactions to the Quakers in "Thoreau Attends Quaker Meeting" (*Friends Intelligencer*, Fifth Month 6, 1944). His attitude toward the Roman Catholics is discussed in Lawrence Willson, "Thoreau and Roman Catholicism" (*CathHR*, XLII, 1956, 157–72). For a discussion of Thoreau as a freethinker, see "An Ideal for Freethinkers" (*Truth Seeker*, June 24, 1893). For an interpretation of him as a Theosophist, see "Theosophist Unaware" (*Theosophy*, 1944, 290–95, 330–34). See also R. W. B. Lewis, *American Adam* (Chicago, 1955).

For Thoreau and the reform movements of his day, see William H. Kirchner, "Henry David Thoreau as a Social Critic" (University of Minnesota, Ph.D., 1938). The most detailed study of his relationship with the abolitionists is Wendell Glick, "Thoreau and Radical Abolitionism" (Northwestern University, Ph.D., 1950). See also Nick Aaron Ford, "Henry David Thoreau, Abolitionist" (*NEQ*, XIX, 1946, 359–71); Walter Harding, "Thoreau and the Negro" (*Negro History Bulletin*, October, 1946); and Howard R. Floan, *The South in Northern Eyes, 1831 to 1861* (Austin, Tex., 1958, pp. 62–70).

On Thoreau's attitude toward government, see the Kirchner dissertation cited above; Eunice M. Schuster, "Native American Anarchism" (*Smith College Studies in History*, XVII, 1931, 46–51); John C. Broderick, "Thoreau's Proposals for Legislation" (*AQ*, VII, 1955, 285–90), and Broderick, "Thoreau's Principle of Simplicity" (University of North Carolina, Ph.D., 1953). See also Charles Madison, "Henry David Thoreau, Transcendental Individualist" in *Critics and Crusaders* (New York, 1947, pp. 174–93); Rudolf Rocker, *Pioneers of American Freedom* (Los Angeles, 1949, 24–31); Charles H. Nichols, "Thoreau on the Citizen and His Government" (*Pylon*, XIII, 1952, 19–24); and Paul H. Oehser, "Pioneers in Conservation" (*Nature Magazine*, XXXVIII, 1945, 188–90).

Thoreau's economic theory is discussed in detail in the Kirchner dissertation cited above; but see also Francis B. Dedmond, "Economic Protest in Thoreau's Journals" (*SN*, XXVI, 1954, 65–76); James Dabbs, "Thoreau, the Adventurer as Economist" (*YR*, XXXVI, 1947, 667–72); and Leo Stoller, "Thoreau's Doctrine of Simplicity" (*NEQ*, XXIX, 1956, 443–61).

For Thoreau's attitude toward civilization and primitivism, see the Broderick dissertation listed above and also John Christie, "Thoreau, Traveler" (Duke University, Ph.D., 1955); Reginald Cook, "The Machine Age and Man" in *Passage to Walden* (Boston, 1949, 99–121); H. S. Canby, "Thoreau and the Machine Age" (*YR*, XX, 1931, 517–31); G. Ferris Cronkhite, "The Transcendental Railroad" (*NEQ*, XXIV, 1951, 306–28); Georges Poulet, *Studies in Human Time*, translated from the French by Elliott Coleman (Baltimore, 1956, pp. 334–37); Kenneth Robinson, "Thoreau and the Wild Appetite" (*TSB* XII); and Mary

Culhane, "Thoreau, Melville, Poe, and the Romantic Quest" (University of Minnesota, Ph.D., 1945).

For Thoreau's ideas on solitude, see particularly Robert Paul Cobb, "Society Versus Solitude: Studies in Emerson, Thoreau, Hawthorne, and Whitman" (University of Michigan, Ph.D., 1955); but see also many of the articles listed in the paragraph above, particularly the Broderick dissertation.

For Thoreau's interest in the pioneer and the Indian, see Lawrence Willson, "The Influence of Early North American History and Legend on the Writings of Henry David Thoreau" (Yale University, Ph.D., 1944); Jason Almus Russell, "Thoreau, the Interpreter of the Real Indian" (*QQ*, XXXV, 1927, 37–48); Arthur Volkman, "Excerpts from Works on Henry David Thoreau" (*Archaeological Society of Delaware Papers*, V, 1943, 1–11), an anthology of Thoreau's comments on the Indian; and studies listed in the Sources for Chapter Three on Thoreau's sources in Indian literature. Thoreau's Indian collections are described in *Reports of the Peabody Museum of American Archaeology and Ethnology* (I, 1876, 6–7). See also Lawrence Willson, "From Thoreau's Indian Manuscripts" (*ESQ*, XI, 1958, 52–55). An important study of Thoreau's Indian notebooks is Lawrence Willson, "Thoreau and the Natural Diet" (*SAQ*, LVII, 1958, 86–103).

The most complete exposition of Thoreau's theory of aesthetics is Charles Reid Metzger, "The Transcendental Esthetics in America" (University of Washington, Ph.D., 1954); but see also the Kirchner dissertation listed above, particularly pp. 177 ff. For an explanation of Thoreau's apparent misinterpretation of Horatio Greenough's aesthetic theories, see William J. Griffin, "Thoreau's Reactions to Horatio Greenough" (*NEQ*, XXX, 1957, 508–12).

The most authoritative discussion of Thoreau's educational theories is Anton M. Huffert, "Thoreau as a Teacher, Lecturer, and Educational Thinker" (New York University, Ph.D., 1951). See also Raymond Adams, "Thoreau, Pioneer in Adult Education" (*Institute Magazine*, III, 1930, 6 ff.); Harry Elmore Hurd, "Henry David Thoreau—A Pioneer in the Field of Education" (*Education*, XLIX, 1929, 372–76); John Dewey, "On Thoreau" (*TSB* 30); the Kirchner dissertation, particularly "The Educational World" (pp. 8–38); and Walter Harding, "Thoreau and the Concord Lyceum" (*TSB* 30).

Harry H. Crosby, "Henry David Thoreau and the Art of Writing" (University of Iowa, M.A., 1947), although very generalized in its approach, lists in the footnotes many of Thoreau's comments on writing. A good brief selection of Thoreau's comments is gathered together in Harrison Hayford and Howard Vincent, *Reader and Writer* (Boston, 1954, 176–78). Edwin Way Teale of Baldwin, N. Y., has made a much fuller compilation, but it is not yet published.

There are two lengthy studies of Thoreau's literary theory: George D. Craig, "Literary Criticism in the Works of Henry David Thoreau" (University of Utah, Ph.D., 1951), and Raymond Adams, "Henry Thoreau's Literary Theory and Criticism" (University of North Carolina, Ph.D., 1928). The latter is the pioneer American dissertation on Thoreau, and, although unpublished, has had a wide influence on all subsequent studies of Thoreau.

The most authoritative study of Thoreau's use of the organic theory is Fred W. Lorch, "Thoreau and the Organic Principle in Poetry" (University of Iowa, Ph.D., 1936), published almost in its entirety in *PMLA* (LIII, 1938, 286–302). There is also a very provocative discussion in F. O. Matthiessen, *American Renaissance* (New York, 1941, *passim*). One should also consult Carl Bode's edition of Thoreau's *Collected Poems* (Chicago, 1943, p. 338).

On Thoreau's style, see J. Brooks Atkinson, "Concerning Thoreau's Style" (*Freeman*, VI, 1922, 8–10); Adaline Conway, *The Essay in American Literature* (New York, 1914, pp. 68–78); F. O. Matthiessen, *American Renaissance* (pp. 92–99); Sherman Paul's introduction to his edition of *Walden* (Boston, 1957); and Walter Harding, "Henry David Thoreau: Philologist" (*WS*, XIX, 1944, 7).

A good discussion of Thoreau's use of humor is Harold N. Guthrie, "The Humor of Thoreau" (University of Iowa, Ph.D., 1953); but see also George Beardsley, "Thoreau as a Humorist" (*Dial*, XXVIII, 1900, 241–43), and James Paul Brawner, "Thoreau as Wit and Humorist" (*SAQ*, XLIV, 1945, 170–76). By far the best discussion of Thoreau's humor is J. Golden Taylor, "Neighbor Thoreau's Critical Humor" (*Utah State University Monograph Series*, VI, 1958), which unfortunately appeared too late to be discussed in this chapter. Raymond Adams discusses Thoreau's use of the mock-heroic in "Thoreau's Mock-Heroics and the American Natural History Writers" (*SP*, LII, 1955, 86–97). A recent and exceptionally good article, although it is by no means exhaustive, is C. Grant Loomis, "Henry David Thoreau as Folklorist" (*WF*, XVI, 1957, 90–106). It should arouse further interest and research in this virtually untouched area of Thoreau's interest.

Works Cited

Harding, Walter. *Thoreau: A Century of Criticism*. Dallas: Southern Methodist University Press, 1954.

Thoreau, Henry David. *A Week on the Concord and Merrimack Rivers, Walden, The Maine Woods, Cape Cod*. New York: The Library of America, 1985.

———. *The Portable Thoreau*. Edited by Carl Bode, New York: Viking Press, 1947.

Chronology

1817	Henry David Thoreau—born David Henry—on July 12 at Concord, Massachusetts.
1828	Enters Concord Academy.
1833	Enters Harvard.
1837	Graduates from Harvard. Begins teaching at the Concord School, but resigns over the issue of corporal punishment. Meets Ralph Waldo Emerson; begins writing his *Journal*.
1838	Starts a private school with his brother John. Gives his first public lecture at the Concord Lyceum.
1839	Canoe trip on the Concord and Merrimack Rivers with his brother John.
1840	Publishes in *The Dial*, the Transcendentalists' new magazine.
1841	Takes up residence at Emerson's home.
1842	Thoreau's brother John dies of lockjaw after cutting his finger while shaving.
1843	Tutors for the family of Emerson's brother William on Staten Island.
1844	Returns home; works at the Thoreau family's pencil-making business.
1845	Begins building a house on the banks of Walden Pond.

1846	Arrested and jailed overnight for refusing to pay the poll tax to a U.S. government that supported slavery.
1847	Leaves Walden Pond and again moves in with the Emersons.
1849	Moves back to his family's home; *A Week on the Concord and Merrimack Rivers* and "Civil Disobedience" are published. Visits Cape Cod.
1850	Travels to Canada.
1854	Publishes *Walden*; delivers "Slavery in Massachusetts" lecture.
1856	Meets Walt Whitman in New York.
1859	Delivers "A Plea for Captain John Brown" lecture.
1861	Moves to Minnesota because of failing health.
1862	Thoreau dies of tuberculosis on May 6.

Works by Henry David Thoreau

BOOKS

A Week on the Concord and Merrimack Rivers. 1849.
Walden; or, Life in the Woods. 1854.

ESSAYS AND OTHER WORKS

"Aulus Persius Flaccus." 1840.

"Natural History of Massachusetts." 1842.

"Homer, Ossian, Chaucer." 1843.

"A Walk to Wachusett." 1843.

"Dark Ages." 1843.

"A Winter Walk." 1843.

"The Landlord." October 1843.

"Herald of Freedom." 1844.

"Thomas Carlyle and His Works." 1847.

"Ktaadn and the Maine Woods." 1848.

"Resistance to Civil Government" (1849) / "Civil Disobedience" (1866).

"The Iron Horse." 1852.

"A Poet Buying a Farm." 1852.

"An Excursion to Canada." 1853.

"A Massachusetts Hermit." 1854.

"Slavery in Massachusetts." 1854.

"The Shipwreck." 1855.

"Stage Coach Views." 1855.

"The Plains of Nanset [sic]." 1855.

"The Beach." 1855.

"Chesuncook." 1858.

"The Last Days of John Brown." 1860.

"A Plea for Captain John Brown." 1860.

"Remarks at Concord on the Day of the Execution of John Brown." 1860.

"The Succession of Forest Trees." 1860.

POSTHUMOUSLY PUBLISHED BOOKS

Excursions. 1863.

The Maine Woods. 1864.

Cape Cod. 1865.

A Yankee in Canada, with Anti-Slavery and Reform Papers. 1866.

POSTHUMOUSLY PUBLISHED ESSAYS

"Walking." 1862.

"Wild Apples." 1862.

"Life Without Principle." 1863.

"Night and Moonlight." 1863.

"The Wellfleet Oysterman." 1864.

"The Highland Light." 1864.

"The Service." 1902.

Miscellaneous Writings

"Paradise (to Be) Regained" [book review]. 1843.

"Wendell Phillips before the Concord Lyceum" [letter to the editor]. 1845.

Works about Henry David Thoreau

Allen, Francis H. *A Bibliography of Henry David Thoreau.* New York: B. Franklin, 1968.

Berger, Michael Benjamin. *Thoreau's Late Career.* London: Camden House, 2000.

Borst, Raymond R. *The Thoreau Log: A Documentary Life of Henry David Thoreau, 1817–1862.* New York: G. K. Hall, 1992.

————. *Henry David Thoreau: A Reference Guide, 1835–1899.* Boston: G. K. Hall, 1987.

Botkin, Daniel. *No Man's Garden: Thoreau and a New Vision for Civilization and Nature.* Washington, D.C.: Island Press, 2000.

Buell, Lawrence. *The Environmental Imagination: Thoreau, Nature Writing, and the Formation of American Culture.* Cambridge, Mass.: Belknap, 1996.

————. *Literary Transcendentalism: Style and Vision in the American Renaissance.* Ithaca: Cornell University Press, 1973.

Cain, William, ed. *Historical Guide to Henry David Thoreau.* Oxford: Oxford University Press, 2000.

Canby, Henry Seidel. *Thoreau.* Gloucester: Peter Smith, 1965.

Cavell, Stanley. *The Senses of Walden.* San Francisco: North Point Press, 1981.

Channing, William Ellery. *Thoreau: The Poet-Naturalist.* Boston: Roberts Brothers, 1873.

The Dictionary of Literary Biography, volume 223. Detroit: Gale Research Group, 2000.

Edel, Leon. *Henry D. Thoreau*. Minneapolis: University of Minnesota Press, 1970.

Gerber, Frederick. *Thoreau's Redemptive Imagination*. New York: New York University Press, 1977.

Hahn, Stephen. *On Thoreau*. Belmont, Calif.: Wadsworth, 1999.

Hanson, Elizabeth. *Thoreau's Indian of the Mind*. New York: Edwin Mellen, 1992.

Harding, Walter. *A Thoreau Handbook*. New York: New York University Press, 1959.

Hendrick, George, Willene Hendrick, Henry S. Salt, and Fritz Oehschlager, eds. *Life of Henry David Thoreau*. Champaign, Ill.: University of Illinois Press, 2000.

Hildebidle, John. *Thoreau, A Naturalist's Liberty*. Cambridge: Harvard University Press, 1983.

Howarth, William L. *The Book of Concord: Thoreau's Life as a Writer*. New York: Viking Press, 1982.

Lowell, James Russell. *Essays, Poems, and Letters*. New York: The Odyssey Press, 1948.

Madden, Edward H. *"Civil Disobedience" and the Moral Law in the Nineteenth Century American Philosophy*. Seattle: University of Washington Press, 1968.

Marx, Leo. *The Machine in the Garden: Technology and the Pastoral Ideal in America*. Oxford: Oxford University Press, 1964.

Mathiessen, F.O. *The American Renaissance: Art and Expression in the Age of Emerson and Whitman*. Oxford: Oxford University Press, 1941.

Miller, Perry. *Nature's Nation*. Cambridge: Harvard University Press, 1967.

Myerson, Joel, ed. *The Cambridge Companion to Henry David Thoreau*. Cambridge: Cambridge University Press, 1995.

———, ed. *Critical Essays on Henry David Thoreau's "Walden"*. Boston: G. K. Hall, 1988.

Paul, Sherman. *Thoreau: A Collection of Critical Essays*. Englewood Cliffs, N.J.: Prentice-Hall, 1962.

Peck, H. Daniel. *Thoreau's Morning Work: Memory and Perception in A Week on the Concord and Merrimack Rivers*. New Haven, Conn.: Yale University Press, 1994.

Richardson, Robert D. *Henry Thoreau: A Life of the Mind*. Berkeley: University of California Press, 1988.

Ruland, Richard, ed. *Twentieth Century Interpretations of Walden: A Collection of Critical Essays*. Englewood Cliffs, N.J.: Prentice-Hall, 1968.

Sayre, Robert F. *Thoreau and the American Indians*. Princeton: Princeton University Press, 1977.

Schneider, Richard J. *Henry David Thoreau*. Boston: Twayne, 1987.

Schneider, Richard J., Wayne Franklin, and Lawrence Buell, eds. *Thoreau's Sense of Place: Essays in American Environmental Writing*. Iowa City: University of Iowa Press, 2000.

Smith, David Clyde. *The Transcendental Saunterer: Thoreau and the Search for Self*. Savannah, Ga.: Frederic C. Beil, 1997.

Smith, Harmon L. *My Friend, My Friend: The Story of Thoreau's Relationship with Emerson*. Boston: University of Massachusetts, 1999.

Spiller, Robert E. *Four Makers of the American Mind*. Durham, N.C.: Duke University Press, 1976.

Stevenson, Robert Louis. *Familiar Studies of Men and Books*. New York: Charles Scribner's Sons, 1924.

Tauber, Alfred. *Henry David Thoreau and the Moral Agency of Knowing*. Berkeley: University of California Press, 2001.

Tripp, Raymond P. *Two Fish on One Hook: A Transformative Reading of Thoreau's* Walden. New York: Lindisfarne, 1998.

Walls, Laura Dassow. *Seeing New Worlds: Henry David Thoreau and Nineteenth-Century Natural Science*. La Crosse, Wis.: University of Wisconsin Press, 1995.

Worley, Sam McGuire. *Emerson, Thoreau, and the Role of the Cultural Critic*. New York: State University of New York Press, 2001.

WEBSITES

Thoreau Reader
  eserver.org/thoreau/
Henry D. Thoreau Home Page
  www.walden.org/thoreau/
Henry David Thoreau—American Transcendentalism Web
  www.vcu.edu/engweb/transcendentalism/authors/thoreau/
Henry David Thoreau
  www.transcendentalists.com/1thorea.html
Perspectives in American Literature: Henry David Thoreau
  www.csustan.edu/english/reuben/pal/chap4/thoreau.html
The Writings of Henry D. Thoreau
  www.niulib.niu.edu/thoreau/

Contributors

HAROLD BLOOM is Sterling Professor of the Humanities at Yale University and Henry W. and Albert A. Berg Professor of English at the New York University Graduate School. He is the author of over 20 books, including *Shelley's Mythmaking* (1959), *The Visionary Company* (1961), *Blake's Apocalypse* (1963), *Yeats* (1970), *A Map of Misreading* (1975), *Kabbalah and Criticism* (1975), *Agon: Toward a Theory of Revisionism* (1982), *The American Religion* (1992), *The Western Canon* (1994), and *Omens of Millennium: The Gnosis of Angels, Dreams, and Resurrection* (1996). *The Anxiety of Influence* (1973) sets forth Professor Bloom's provocative theory of the literary relationships between the great writers and their predecessors. His most recent books include *Shakespeare: The Invention of the Human* (1998), a 1998 National Book Award finalist, *How to Read and Why* (2000), and *Genius: A Mosaic of One Hundred Exemplary Creative Minds* (2002). In 1999, Professor Bloom received the prestigious American Academy of Arts and Letters Gold Medal for Criticism, and in 2002 he received the Catalonia International Prize.

ELLYN SANNA has authored more than 50 books, including adult non-fiction, novels, young adult biographies, and gift books. She also works as a freelance editor and manages Scrivener's Ink, an editorial service.

MICHAEL CISCO is a graduate student in the English department of New York University, and author of *The Divinity Student*.

America's pre-eminent nineteenth-century philosopher, RALPH WALDO EMERSON (1803–1882) was America's principal ambassador of Transcendentalism and a poet, essayist, and lecturer of unparalleled influence in American thought. In his popular lectures, which would later become essays in widely read collections, the first of which was simply entitled *Nature*, he quietly proclaimed an individualistic philosophy which drew some of the brightest minds in American history into his circle.

DR. WALTER HARDING'S biographies and critical studies of Thoreau have become the indispensable core texts of any serious student of Thoreau. Founder and president of the Thoreau Society, founded in 1941, he taught at the State University of New York at Geneseo for over thirty years, retiring as a Distinguished Professor Emeritus of American Literature.

Index